SALADS

Peter Gordon
SALADS
the new main course

PHOTOGRAPHY BY JEAN CAZALS

INTRODUCTION 7
INCLUDING THE ELEMENTS OF THE IDEAL SALAD, ADDING CRUNCH AND A DISCUSSION OF DRESSINGS

First published in 2005 by
Quadrille Publishing Limited,
Alhambra House, 27–31 Charing Cross
Road, London WC2H 0LS

Editorial Director: Jane O'Shea
Creative Director: Helen Lewis
Editor & Project Manager: Lewis Esson
Art Director: Lawrence Morton
Photography: Jean Cazals
Food Styling: Peter Gordon
Styling: Sue Rowlands
Production: Beverley Richardson

Cataloguing in Publication Data:
a catalogue record for this
book is available from the
British Library

ISBN 1 84400 140 7

Printed and bound by Best Tri

Introduction

I'm a huge fan of the salad. While I prefer cooking for friends at home, more than in any other cooking situation, I have to admit that I don't do it nearly as much as I wish I could. Almost all of the food I cook and prepare is created at our restaurant, served to customers. In a restaurant situation, apart from simple side salads, a salad has to be as exciting as any other dish on the menu. Our guests at The Providores and Tapa Room restaurants always expect to be served a flavourful and exciting meal. Guests often order our starter salads for their main course and it's this fact that made me realise that there is a whole world of possibilities for this menu item to be served as a main course. Jane O'Shea from Quadrille and my editor Lewis Esson also had the same thoughts, hence this book.

In summertime it's fairly common to serve a salad as a main course as the heat can sometimes make preparing and eating a cooked meal exhausting. However, there are also salads in this book that make perfect autumn and winter meals, using much heartier ingredients than the usual summer vegetables and salad leaves. I had a lot of fun creating and writing these recipes – they have all been cooked and tested by me in my kitchen at home – so I hope you'll try them out and enjoy them as much as I have with friends in your own home.

THE ELEMENTS OF THE IDEAL SALAD

What exactly is a salad? Is it merely a few raw ingredients tossed together in a bowl with a dressing, or is it more complex than that? For my purposes in writing this book, I have taken the view that a salad is a mixture of ingredients, individually prepared (as opposed to being cooked together in a stew), that all work in harmony with each other, some simply tossed together and others arranged on a plate. Some are just assemblages of delicious ingredients, each looking after itself, and some are great swathes of ingredients working together to create a meal in one.

The idea of harmony is itself up for discussion. In fact, to create harmony you sometimes need to generate chaos or a clash of some sort. Adding a contrasting flavour or texture to a mix can often highlight other ingredients in the same dish. In the following recipes you'll discover that it might be the shock of a sweet roast sultana that highlights sharp citrus notes, or a spicy chilli that adds warmth to a sweet dessert.

A salad likes to have texture complexity. Whether this is derived from a crunchy texture due to the addition of nuts and croutons, or a soft texture from buffalo mozzarella or yoghurt, you need to offer more than one texture in a salad. Much as a tender green salad with a little olive oil and lemon juice makes a great starter or side dish, it won't leave your dinner guests contented. However, add some sliced pear and roasted hazelnuts, a few green beans and maybe some shaved Parmesan, and then you're talking.

What is important in creating a salad is that the produce you use is of premium quality – perhaps more so in salads than in cooked dishes, as they are often given little further treatment. Often you'll be serving just five or six ingredients mixed together with a dressing, and if just one of those ingredients doesn't taste that great you can very easily ruin the whole salad.

Choose salad leaves that are plump and firm – no wilted ones please (although a quick dip in cold water, a shake to dry them and then an hour in a plastic bag in the fridge can sometimes work wonders with greens and herbs).

Choose fruit and vegetables that are in season and in their prime. If you use a tomato in the middle of winter, then don't expect it to taste like the summer ones you had on holiday in the countryside. Likewise, if it's December in Europe and you want to make a cold strawberry salad for the Christmas table, then I'd advise you to choose a new recipe rather than buy some much-travelled berries.

SALADS THAT SATISFY

Apart from those featured in the first and last chapters, of course, all of the salads in the book are designed to be served to 4 people as a main course. Most will also work as starters – just make them smaller, or use the quantities given to feed 6–8 people as a first course.

There will, of course, be some people (like my father) to whom they will be too small as a main course, and some diners may want to know where the meat is (look at the meat chapters) – but then I suppose this book may not be for them. I'll write a meat book next!

However, I wanted to create a book of recipes that would inspire you to have the confidence to create an exciting meal just by looking at the ingredients you probably already have to hand in the fridge, or at least are available from your local shops. Admittedly, some recipes call for more preparation than others (preparing artichokes is well worth the final effort), but you can also use pre-prepared alternatives (for example, artichoke hearts in olive oil are mostly good) from many stores. Where I can, I've offered advice on alternative ingredients, and if you'd prefer to use, say, frozen broad beans instead of fresh, then do so. Cooking should be fun, not a tedious chore.

LIBERAL QUANTITIES

I have taken quite a casual approach to the measures of ingredients. When assessing how much rocket it would require to feed 4 people I decided that '1 or 2 handfuls' was far easier and more realistic a quantity than '100 grams' or '1 bunch' (how big a bunch will depend on where you bought it from). Likewise a cup of some ingredients can prove confusing. One cup of olives – if the olives are jumbo black olives from Greece – will give you around 12; a cup of small Arbequina olives from Catalonia will give you almost 30. So I've opted for 'handfuls' of olives, capers and similar ingredients – and you will have to decide how much you actually want.

SEASONING SENSIBILITIES

This is another very personal area. I find that I have a low tolerance to salt and tend to season on the light side, but at no loss to flavour as far as I'm concerned. However, I have friends who adore salt – so how best to cater for them? I simply season dishes as I like them and put salt on the table. You can always add more salt to a finished dish, but you can't remove it. When I ask you to season a salad, then you will have to decide how much to put in.

It's worth noting that miso (fermented rice and soya bean paste), soy sauce and fish sauce are also good seasoning agents. They will, though, darken a dressing, and therefore the salad itself, as well as adding their own individual flavour.

Regarding pepper, I think there's little excuse for using ready-ground pepper these days. A grinder will last a lifetime and most stores sell reasonably inexpensive ones. Some large stores even sell peppercorns in disposable grinders – a little wasteful to my taste, but certainly a good way to introduce someone to the joys of freshly milled pepper.

Chillies, while not being an everyday seasoning (unless you happen to live with me), are also up for discussion regarding intensity. The rule of thumb is that a small wrinkly chilli will be hotter than a medium smooth chilli. It's the seeds and the fibres holding these to the body that create most of the heat. If unsure how hot a chilli is, remove the green stem, cut the chilli in half lengthways and scrape out the seeds and pale membrane with a small teaspoon – running it lengthways down the chilli. Add the body, usually chopped, to the dish and taste. If it needs more heat, add a little of the chopped seeds and fibre – go gently and you'll be fine. It pays to wear gloves when preparing chillies, as they linger on your fingers. Unless I've specified it, don't remove the seeds, and I have assumed the chillies you use will be medium in strength – use more or less to taste.

ADDING 'CRUNCH'

As I've said, 'texture' is all-important in salads. It's perhaps a more Asian approach to creating food than is evident in classic European cuisine, but it all adds to the final memory of a dish. Here are some tips for adding interesting crunch and flavours to your salads.

Soy sunflower seeds: These have their roots in macrobiotic cooking; in fact my partner, Michael, learned how to make them when he was macrobiotic almost 25 years ago. Heat a heavy-based fry pan and add a large handful of sunflower seeds. Toast in the pan, shaking and stirring frequently over moderate heat, until they colour. Add 2 tablespoons of soy sauce or tamari (wheat-free soy sauce) and cook to evaporate it, stirring constantly. Once the liquid has all gone, tip the seeds on to a plate and leave to cool. Separate any seeds that have joined together and store in an airtight jar.

Sesame seeds: Toasted sesame seeds add a really lovely savoury taste to a salad, as well as a mouth-popping texture. Toasting them can be messy, though, as they pop all over the stovetop. You can do one of two things: either roast them in the oven at 160°C, gas 3, until golden, or toast them in small amounts in a pan with a lid. Shake them over moderate heat and, when most are golden-brown, tip them out to cool.

Spiced popcorn: Popcorn in salads may seem too odd. However, I was adding such a thing to salads at The Sugar Club Restaurant in New Zealand in 1988, and recently our sous-chef at The Providores, the fabulous Miles Kirby, did the same thing with his salad of blue cheese, popcorn, chilli and herbs.

Heat a deep pot, which has a tight-fitting lid, to hotter than moderate. Add a scant teaspoon of groundnut, refined olive or avocado oil, and add a small handful of popcorn kernels (make sure you buy the correct stuff). Shake the pan every now and then until you hear the corn begin to pop, then gently shake it continuously, never taking it off the heat, until the popping stops. Tip the corn into a bowl and place the pan back on the heat with another scant teaspoon of oil. Add a few pinches of chilli flakes, cayenne or paprika, cumin, ajowan or

caraway seeds, coarsely ground coriander seeds or green cardamom seeds, finely chopped garlic or chilli, and quickly sizzle over the heat, then pour on the corn and toss together with 1/2 teaspoon of sugar. Store in an airtight jar once cooled, and eat within 48 hours.

Sesame Rice Crackers (see above): Place 3/4 cup sticky (glutinous) rice and 2 cups of water in a small non-stick pan and bring to the boil, stirring continuously. Put on a tight-fitting lid and gently simmer for 20 minutes. Take off the heat and mix in 2 teaspoons each Thai fish sauce (or a little salt) and black sesame seeds. Spread on a tray lined with baking parchment, sit another sheet on top and roll out to 3-4mm thick. Peel off the top parchment and let cool completely. Cut into strips or discs and sit these on some clean parchment, then leave to firm up. Once stiff, sit them on a rack in an airy place until rock hard. To finish, heat 3cm of oil to 180°C and fry the crackers until puffed up on both sides. Drain on kitchen paper and store in an airtight jar for up to 3 days.

Croutons: Croutons are a great salad addition in that they both use up leftovers and provide a delicious crunch – one that crumbles in your mouth as you eat it. Simply slice or dice leftover stale bread (it'll be easier to slice if it is more than 2 days old) and toss or brush with enough extra-virgin olive oil (or nut oil) barely to coat. For a handful of 1cm diced croutons you'd need 1 1/2 tablespoons of oil. For sliced croutons, it's easier to lay them on a baking tray and then either drizzle or brush the oil over them. Don't pile them on

top of each other or they won't cook evenly. Bake in an oven preheated to 170°C, gas 3½ until golden. You can also fry them in oil, but they will absorb more oil.

Crispy shallots and garlic: These two ingredients are very Southeast Asian and lovely in salads with garlic in the dressing or those with a lot of fresh herbs. The best shallots to use are the small red Thai ones.

For the garlic, simply peel the cloves and thinly. For the shallots, peel and thinly slice, then toss with a little salt to absorb some of the moisture and leave for 30 minutes (use 1 teaspoon of salt for each handful of sliced shallots). Gently squeeze excess moisture from them, rinse briefly under cold water and gently squeeze dry again, then pat dry on kitchen paper. Place the sliced garlic or shallots into a wok or a pan and cover with 4cm of vegetable oil. Turn the heat to medium and, once the pan begins to heat up, begin stirring the garlic or shallots to prevent sticking. Once they begin to sizzle, keep an eye on them; and once they've gone to just beyond golden, remove them with a slotted spoon and drain on kitchen paper. Once cooled and crisp, store in airtight containers.

You can buy these ready-made in Asian stores. Indian shops also sell crispy onions cooked this way, which are great sprinkled over meat-based salads.

Toasted nuts: Nuts are perhaps the most commonly used crunchy ingredient. The rule of thumb when toasting them is never to mix different types of nut on the same tray as they cook at different speeds. Set your oven to 160°C, gas 3, lay the nuts on a tray and bake until they colour to a good golden brown. Shake them from time to time to ensure that they colour evenly. After you take them from the oven, they will continue to cook for a few minutes more, so keep an eye on them as a burnt nut can easily ruin a salad. A pine nut will take about 8–10 minutes to toast, a cashew about 15. You can also cook nuts in a dry pan but I find this less effective, and often the nut will burn in patches yet still be raw on the inside.

If the nuts have skin on them (often how you buy hazelnuts), toast them as described above and, once they've coloured, tip them into a tea towel and wrap them up. The steam generated in the towel loosens the skin and, once they've cooled down to a comfortable temperature, rub them together for a minute or so, in the towel, and the skins come off easily.

Caramelized crisp nuts: This method produces delicious shiny sweet, crunchy cashews and peanuts. Place a large handful of skinless nuts in a pot and pour on a litre of cold water with a teaspoon of salt. Bring to the boil and boil cashews for 5 minutes or peanuts for 8. Drain in a colander, then tip into a bowl, add 3 tablespoons of sugar and toss to coat. Tip on to a tray lined with non-stick baking parchment and leave to cool and dry (you want the sugar to form a coating on the nuts; they must be dry when you fry them). This can take overnight in a breezy or warm place (an airing cupboard is good, but make sure you keep away from moisture. If in a hurry, you can also dry them in an oven set low to 100°C, gas ¼. Once they've dried out, separate any that have stuck together. Heat a wok or pot with 3cm of groundnut oil (or other suitable cooking oil) to around 170°C and add one-third of the nuts. Cook, stirring constantly, until they are a medium caramel colour – make sure you don't overcook them, as they will continue to cook a little when you take them out. Remove with a slotted spoon, place on non-stick parchment and leave to cool. Don't do as I once did and lay them on kitchen paper – the caramel coating will stick to it and it's impossible to remove. Leave to cool and store in an airtight jar.

A DISCUSSION OF DRESSINGS

It is often the dressing that either makes or breaks a salad. A simple dressing helps moisten the dish, but a well-balanced dressing with layers of flavour can itself be the highlight of the experience. A dressing has to be in balance. That means the acidity and the oiliness need to work in harmony. However, you also need to bear in mind the components of the dish. For example, if you're using chunks of citrus fruit or grapes roasted with verjuice or tamarind, then you need to make a dressing that edges back from being too acidic or it'll make the whole dish way too sharp. Likewise, if making a dressing to go with something like artichokes braised in olive oil, go for one that isn't too oily or you might drown the dish. When making the dressing, you can either whisk everything together in a small bowl, or even easier is to put them in a jar, screw the lid on and shake it all together.

Acidity and oil ratio: I generally use 3–4 parts of oil to 1 part vinegar. To make enough dressing for 4 large green salads, use 5 tablespoons extra-virgin olive oil to just less than $1\frac{1}{2}$ tablespoons cider or balsamic vinegar. If using lemon juice, pomegranate molasses or verjuice instead of vinegar, then use a slightly higher ratio of acidic component (around 3.5 to 1.5) as all three are less acidic than vinegar.

Acidity and sourness: The range of vinegars available these days is incredible. When I was a kid, all I knew was malt, white and – still my favourite – cider vinegar. In my local deli the other day, I counted over 15 types, including sherry vinegar (regular and PX – made from the dried sultana-tasting Pedro Ximenez grape), red wine vinegar from three different countries, apple vinegar of three types (organic and non-), rice vinegar and three types of balsamic, ranging in price from a few pounds to £30 a bottle... So many to chose from and all with differing characteristics.

To make matters worse, you can also add acidity and sourness by means of other ingredients. My favourites are pomegranate molasses (also great drizzled over ice cream), verjuice (made from unfermented grapes and needing to be kept in the fridge once opened), tamarind (you can extract the sourness yourself by squashing the pulp of the fruit in warm water then passing through a sieve – or buy the inferior ready-made paste) and the juice of citrus fruit – from lemons to grapefruit, oranges and clementines. Remember, too, that it's not just the juice from citrus fruit that will give flavour to a salad – the finely grated zest will also add character. If you can find unwaxed fruit, these are preferable. However, chances are the fruit you buy will have a fine layer of wax sprayed on them to preserve them – you'll need to rub this off with a warm cloth or kitchen paper before grating.

OIL BASICS

With regards to the oil you use in the dressing, there are so many to choose from. The less flavoursome, plainer ones – and, therefore, those to use when you want the 'salad ingredients' to stand out – are sunflower, grapeseed, light olive oil and what is often termed ' vegetable salad oil'.

Nut oils – most commonly walnut, hazelnut, almond and peanut (also called groundnut oil) – add flavour, although almond and peanut oils are very subtle. There are also toasted nut oils on the market which have a more pronounced flavour, sometimes a little overbearing in a dressing – so it's often wise to dilute them with a plain oil. Sesame oil has a wonderful flavour (with toasted sesame oil being very intense), but you do need to use it sparingly.

Argan oil is still very rarely used but is absolutely delicious. It's expensive, but the process by which it is produced in Morocco is incredibly time-consuming, involving hand-picking from thorny trees. If you see it and feel like splashing out, then do try it in a simple dressing for green leaves – I guarantee you'll be intrigued by its sweet nutty flavour.

Information on olive oils could – and does – readily fill a book in itself. Very basically, an extra-virgin olive oil has much lower acidity than virgin or 'plain' olive oil. An extra-virgin olive oil begins to lose its grassy fresh flavours after 12–18 months, so try to buy a new season's oil that has been dated, so you aren't disappointed when you drizzle it over your salad.

A brilliant newcomer to the oil world is **avocado oil**. This is produced by crushing avocado flesh and extracting the oil. New Zealand, my home country, is producing the best examples of this and it's becoming more readily available worldwide. It's also great to cook with, as it has a high smoke point (meaning the flavour doesn't taste burnt or deteriorate as it gets hot), so it's perfect for frying fish fillets or chicken breasts, barbecuing and roasting. Not surprisingly, it also works well with any salad that has avocado in it and is great mixed into guacamole. If you find it too strong to use on its own (in fact the same goes with any flavoursome oil) then dilute it with the same amount of a plain oil.

In the oil world, there has been a lot of flavour-adding going on and, mostly, this is a positive thing. You can now buy oils flavoured with chilli, lemon, lime, herbs, garlic and numerous other ingredients, but do bear in mind that they won't all taste great. You'll need to experiment at your own cost – or try oils that friends have already bought.

With all flavoursome oils, it's fairly important to keep them in a cool place, away from any heat, and to use them up fairly quickly. I was once given a 2-litre tin of the most delicious extra-virgin olive oil and immediately decanted it from its fabulous painted Spanish tin into four 500ml dark-glass bottles, which I then sealed. This prevented the oil from oxidizing and deteriorating in flavour.

SOME MORE USEFUL DRESSINGS

Every salad in this book has its own dressing but I wanted to give you a few more current favourites that you might want to try. They will make enough for 4 people and can be used to dress a green salad or even as a dressing over grilled fish or a roast chicken, tossed with steamed vegetables or the like.

SHERRY VINEGAR AND POMEGRANATE MOLASSES DRESSING

1 tablespoon sherry vinegar

2 teaspoons pomegranate molasses

5 tablespoons extra-virgin olive oil

1/2 teaspoon soy sauce

Mix everything together.

SESAME, RICE VINEGAR AND MISO DRESSING

1 teaspoon toasted sesame oil

4 tablespoons sunflower oil

1 1/2 tablespoons rice vinegar

juice of 1 lime

1 teaspoon tahini paste

1 teaspoon miso

1 teaspoon toasted sesame seeds

Mix everything together.

PIMENTON (SMOKED PAPRIKA), GARLIC, THYME AND OLIVE OIL DRESSING

1/2 teaspoon pimenton dulce (sweet smoked paprika)

1 garlic clove, finely chopped

1/2 teaspoon fresh thyme leaves

5 tablespoons extra-virgin olive oil

1 1/2 tablespoons red wine vinegar

2 pinches of salt

Place the pimenton, garlic, thyme and 2 tablespoons of the oil in a small pan and place over a moderate heat. Cook, stirring continuously, until the garlic has coloured slightly.

Add the vinegar and salt, bring to the boil, then tip into a bowl or jar and stir in the remaining oil.

YOGHURT, HAZELNUT OIL, APPLE AND LEMON DRESSING

5 tablespoons natural unsweetened and unflavoured yoghurt

2 tablespoons lemon juice

2 tablespoons apple juice

1 teaspoon English mustard

2 teaspoons hazelnut oil

Mix everything together.

MICROGREEN MAGIC

Throughout this book I list in the ingredients sprouts and cress – and usually suggest you use whatever you have at hand. When I was doing my apprenticeship, I used to sprout mung beans, fenugreek seeds and mustard cress at home for my salads. These days, however, the variety available through farmers markets, supermarkets, food halls and better vegetable suppliers is extraordinary. Throughout the book you'll see rocket cress, basil cress, coriander cress and new sprouts such as China Rose, Buck Sorrel, Russian Cress and numerous others.

While many of these will be hard to track down, you can in fact grow sprouts yourself at home. When sprouting any seeds or grains the worse thing you can do is let them get waterlogged, as they will rot. So make sure you keep them moist but not drowned in water.

Head to your local health food store and chances are they will have special jars for growing the likes of mung bean and chickpea sprouts. These tend to be jars with a mesh lid that screws on. You put the grains in the jar and soak them overnight. Next day, drain the water from the jar and then begin a daily routine of wetting the grains and draining them. Eventually they'll sprout and you'll be able to eat this nutritious food source. Such sprouting jars should come complete with their own instructions.

Mustard cress is grown differently, and you can also use this method for growing the herb cresses (basil, coriander, shiso, fenugreek, parsley). Line a soufflé dish or ramekin with cotton wool (cotton-wool pads are a good fit too) and dampen with water. Sprinkle generously with seeds (too few and they find it hard to grow straight) and leave in a sunlight-filled place (but not in direct sunlight). Next day, moisten the cotton again. This now goes on for up to 3 weeks. Once the seeds sprout, they will quickly shoot up, but you want them to be at least 5cm tall before you snip them at the base.

Microgreen is really just a fancy word for a baby salad leaf. The name seems to have originated in America and I can still remember seeing my first examples of them when I went for a job interview at the Sign of the Dove restaurant in New York in 1988. The salad chef had the most tiny frisée, rocket, red oak leaf and sorrel imaginable. He also had baby beetroot leaves and baby silverbeet. I was absolutely gobsmacked that they could be so small. These days, anyone with a garden or even a window box can grow them. Sow your seeds a little denser than normal and, when they have grown somewhere between 5–8cm, cut them 1cm from the base. Use as soon as possible and store in an airtight bag in the fridge.

Canapé Salads

as party finger food,
often on slices of bread
or in leaf containers

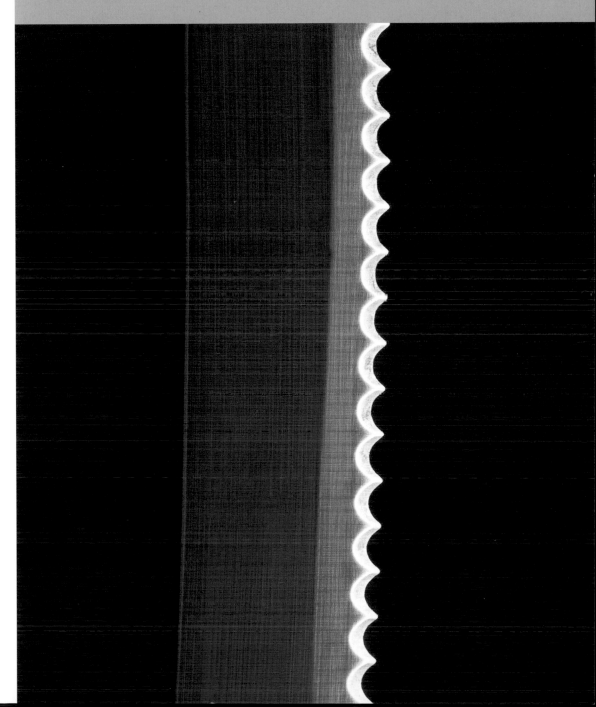

SALMON, MINT AND CUCUMBER SALAD ON CROSTINI

This salad can be made in a jiffy, and you can use pretty much any fish you like – just make sure it's really fresh! As the fish is cut quite small, you need to serve it within 30 minutes of mixing it all together or it will cure too much. What happens is that the citrus juice cures the fish protein, chemically 'cooking' it, changing the colour, texture and flavour to very much that of cooked fish.

The bloodline of a fish is that part of the flesh immediately under the skin, towards the centre, which is darker in colour. Although it's absolutely fine to eat, the colour will make this salad look less enticing.

makes 20

20 thin slices of baguette or similar-sized pieces of your preferred bread

2 tablespoons extra-virgin olive oil

10cm piece of cucumber

juice of 1 large juicy lime (or 2 tablespoons lemon juice)

300g fresh salmon fillet, skin, bloodline (see above) and any pin bones removed

1 spring onion, thinly sliced

12 mint leaves, finely shredded

3 good pinches of sea salt

cress for garnish

Preheat the oven to 170°C, gas 3½. Make the crostini by laying the sliced bread on a baking tray and brushing it with the oil. Bake until golden, turning over halfway through. This will take between 10 and 15 minutes, depending on the bread you're using. Leave to cool on the tray, then store in an airtight container for up to 1 week.

Peel the cucumber, then slice it lengthways and scoop out and discard the seeds. Cut the flesh into narrow strips, then cut these across into dice. Place in a bowl and mix with the lime or lemon juice.

Cut the salmon into similarly sized dice and add to the cucumber together with the spring onion, mint and salt. Mix gently, cover and place in the fridge. Leave to cure for at least 15 minutes, then mix again and taste and adjust the seasoning.

To serve, divide the salad among the crostini and sit some cress on top.

COUSCOUS, BASIL, CUMIN AND TOMATO SALAD
IN VINE LEAVES WITH LEMON YOGHURT DIP

Based on traditional dolmades (Turkish and Greek stuffed vine leaves, with either a vegetarian or minced lamb stuffing), this recipe is a simple-to-make snack that is delicious served as a cocktail canapé. It's important that you use the best-quality vine leaves as they can sometimes be quite salty or taste too strongly of vinegar. Use the smaller ones for this dish; or, if you have to use large ones, first cut out their tough veins before rolling them up.

makes 12

100g couscous (use the instant type to save time)

150ml tomato juice, at room temperature

1 tablespoon extra-virgin olive oil

½ teaspoon cumin seeds

4 sun-dried tomatoes in oil, drained and finely chopped

handful of basil, finely shredded or torn

12 medium-sized vine leaves, patted dry

for the lemon yoghurt dip

125ml thick Greek-style yoghurt

1 tablespoon extra-virgin olive oil

finely grated zest and juice of 1 medium lemon

handful of parsley, finely chopped

Put the couscous in a bowl, pour on the tomato juice and mix well.

In a small pan, heat the olive oil with the cumin seeds until they colour a little, then pour the contents of the pan over the couscous. Add the sun-dried tomatoes and basil, and mix everything together. Cover with cling film and leave for 20 minutes.

Before using the stuffing, mix again thoroughly, then taste and adjust the seasoning, if necessary. Lay one vine leaf on a board at a time, pointed end facing away from you. Place a good spoonful of the mixture in the centre, then form it into a sausage shape running left to right. Roll the end of the leaf closest to you over the mixture, then fold in both sides towards the centre. Roll the 'sausage' away from you, keeping it firm. Place on a tray with the seam of the pointed leaf on the bottom to help it keep rolled. Continue to roll the remaining stuffed leaves.

Cover with cling film and place in the fridge for at least an hour to firm up. Serve within 3 hours.

Meanwhile, make the dip by mixing all the ingredients with a little salt to taste.

To serve, place the dolmades on a platter with the bowl of dip.

BEETROOT, ORANGE AND HAZELNUT SALAD IN CHICORY LEAVES WITH FROMAGE FRAIS

The leaves of chicory (also called whitlof or witloof), like those of Baby Little Gem, were made to be canapé vessels, as they have a natural hollow. You may like to make a platter up using alternating red and green chicory for a lovely effect.

You can use pre-cooked beetroot to save time, but beets you cook yourself will be much nicer. When they're in season, use golden or striped beets, and even blood oranges, for a different look.

Preheat the oven to 200°C, gas 6. Wash the beetroot skins without tearing them, then wrap them tightly in a piece of foil, making sure there isn't a tear in it, as this will let out the steam. Bake on a tray for 60–80 minutes until you can insert a sharp knife through the foil and into the centre of the beets. Leave to cool completely. Remove the foil and, wearing gloves, rub (or peel) the skin off. Cut the beets into 1cm dice and put in a bowl.

Finely grate 1 teaspoon of zest from the orange and put this in another bowl, then segment the orange (see page 150), cut each segment into quarters, and add to the bowl of orange zest together with the lemon juice.

Flatten the nuts with the side of a large knife to crush them a little and mix these and the olive oil into the orange mixture. Season with salt and pepper.

Divide the fromage frais between the chicory leaves and spoon in the orange salad, then add the beetroot dice, leaving any beetroot juice behind as it won't look good dribbling down your chin and on to your best shirt. Sprinkle with the chives.

makes 12

2 medium beetroot (the size of a tomato)

1 large orange

juice of 1 large juicy lemon

24 skinned hazelnuts, toasted until golden

1 tablespoon lemon-flavoured extra-virgin olive oil (see page 14)

salt and freshly ground black pepper

3 tablespoons fromage frais

12 chicory leaves

1 tablespoon thinly sliced chives

WATERMELON, FETA AND BASIL SALAD WITH PUMPKIN SEEDS ON PRAWN CRACKERS

Without the prawn crackers, this is in itself a delicious summer salad – served as a light main course, or as a side dish at a barbecue. Presented like this, however, on cooked Indonesian krupuk udang, the original prawn crackers, it becomes an altogether different taste sensation. You'll be able to find uncooked krupuk in any Chinatown, but you may prefer just to buy the pre-cooked ones from larger supermarkets or, again, Chinatown.

makes 12

vegetable oil for frying

12 krupuk udang or prawn crackers (see above)

small handful of pumpkin seeds

1 tablespoon extra-virgin olive oil

300g watermelon flesh, seeds removed if preferred

120g feta cheese

8 large basil leaves, shredded

1 tablespoon lemon juice

sprouts (see page 16) to garnish (I used coriander sprouts)

Heat 3cm of oil in a pot or deep-fryer to 180°C and cook the prawn crackers until evenly puffed. It will pay to cook them 3–4 at a time. Remove from the oil and drain well on kitchen paper.

Place the pumpkin seeds and olive oil in a small pan and cook over a moderate heat to colour the seeds, stirring often. Tip on to a plate and leave to cool.

Cut the watermelon into small dice and place in a bowl. Crumble in the feta, add the basil and lemon juice, and gently toss together.

To serve, divide the mixture between the prawn crackers and top with the toasted seeds and some sprouts.

CAPE GOOSEBERRY, SMOKED DUCK, SUNFLOWER SEED, YOGHURT AND CHIVE SALAD ON DEEP-FRIED TORTILLA CRISPS

The cape gooseberry or physalis, a native of Peru, is related to that other husky fruit from Mexico, the tomatillo. Funnily enough, they're often called golden tomatoes in the USA and seem to be treated as a savoury item, whereas in the UK they're seen as a fruit.

You can save time deep-frying the tortillas by buying corn chips, or you can bake tortillas in the oven as you would a crostini or crouton.

Cut each tortilla into 6 wedges. Heat 3cm of oil in a saucepan and cook the tortilla wedges until golden and crisp on both sides, then remove with a slotted spoon to drain on kitchen paper and lightly sprinkle with salt.

Heat another small saucepan and add the olive oil followed by the sunflower seeds and cook over a moderate heat, stirring continuously, to colour the seeds a good golden brown. Add the soy sauce (which will spit a little) and then cook, stirring, until that has all evaporated. Tip out on a plate and leave to cool.

Cut the cape gooseberries into quarters and place in a bowl with the sunflower seeds, the duck or chicken slices and the chives. Gently mix together.

To serve, dollop a little of the yoghurt on each tortilla crisp and then spoon the salad on top of that.

makes 12

two 15–20cm round flour tortillas

vegetable oil for frying

salt

1 tablespoon extra-virgin olive oil

medium handful of sunflower seeds

2 teaspoons soy sauce

18 cape gooseberries, husks removed and rinsed

1 boneless smoked duck (or chicken) breast, very thinly sliced

2 tablespoons finely chopped chives

2 tablespoons thick Greek-style yoghurt

This salad also makes a great ravioli filling and goes well with grilled mackerel, salmon or tuna as a salsa to accompany a main course. Versatile stuff! If you can't find Pecorino Sardo (aged firm Pecorino), use Parmesan or some other firm tasty cheese.

For the polenta, I would use the instant type rather than the traditional 'cook-for-45-minutes-while-stirring' variety that I used to use when I started my apprenticeship 23 years ago! It is hard to make the exact amount of polenta for just 12 canapés – this quantity will make more than you need, but you could always use the rest grilled and topped with a tomato and basil salad as a starter for you next dinner party! Or just make more topping and eat it all up.

Line a shallow baking tray about 20cm square with non-stick baking parchment. Bring the water or vegetable stock to the boil with some salt and reduce the heat to a produce a rapid simmer. Whisk in the polenta in a continuous stream, then change your whisk for a spoon and cook for 1 minute, stirring all the time. Add the butter and sesame seeds and continue to cook until the butter is absorbed. Turn the polenta out on the tray and, using a palette knife, spread it out to an even thickness of about 7mm. Leave to cool completely, then cut into whatever shapes you like, either with a knife or a cookie cutter.

Preheat a warm oven. Heat 3cm of oil in a pan and fry the polenta shapes in batches, until golden and crisp on both sides, then place in the warm oven to keep hot.

Place the olive oil in a moderately hot pan and cook the anchovies, mashing them with the back of a spoon as they cook, until they are almost dissolved. Add the diced courgette and continue to cook and stir until they have just begun to soften. Add the lemon zest and juice, and cook for another minute. Take off the heat and leave to cool a little, then mix in the spring onion, cheese and basil.

Divide the mixture between the polenta shapes and serve while still warm.

COURGETTE, ANCHOVY, PECORINO AND BASIL SALAD ON CRISPY SESAME POLENTA

makes 12

320ml water or vegetable stock

salt

80g polenta grains, sieved

25g butter, at room temperature, or 1½ tablespoons extra-virgin olive oil

2 tablespoons toasted sesame seeds (I used a mixture of brown and black seeds)

vegetable oil for frying

1 tablespoon extra-virgin olive oil

2 salted anchovies, or 4 drained anchovy fillets in oil, roughly chopped

1 large courgette, cut into 1cm dice

¼ teaspoon finely grated lemon zest and 2 teaspoons lemon juice

1 spring onion, thinly sliced

80g Pecorino Sardo, coarsely grated

handful of basil leaves, torn or shredded

SPICED ALMOND, GREEN MANGO, MINT, BLACK BEAN AND MOZZARELLA SALAD IN BABY LITTLE GEM LEAVES

Baby Little Gem leaves make a perfect vessel for a canapé – especially the inner ones, when they aren't too floppy. You should get around 6–10 good leaves per lettuce. If you can't get a green mango use half regular mango and half cucumber or jícama, or try green papaya. The black beans are Chinese, and the ones you want to look for are salted whole beans, rather than black bean sauce – although the latter will do at a pinch.

makes 12

handful of almonds (I prefer the ones with the brown skin still on)

1/4 teaspoon pimenton (smoked paprika – picante will be hotter than dulce)

1 teaspoon icing sugar

2 1/2 teaspoons extra-virgin olive oil

1/8 teaspoon salt

1/2 green mango

12 large mint leaves, shredded

juice of 1 lime

1 tablespoon salted black beans (see above), briefly rinsed and drained

150g mozzarella, cut into 1cm dice

2 Baby Gem lettuces, leaves separated (you want 12 good leaves)

Preheat the oven to 160°C, gas 3, and line a baking tray with baking parchment. Mix the almonds with the paprika, icing sugar, 1/2 teaspoon of the olive oil and the salt, and spread on the lined tray. Bake for 15–20 minutes, until the almonds have begun to turn golden on the inside (break one open), then tip on to a plate and leave to cool. Cut each one in half lengthways.

Peel the mango and cut the flesh into fine julienne strips (a mandolin grater is ideal for this). Mix these with the mint and lime juice.

Roughly chop the black beans and mix with the mozzarella.

Divide the mango mixture between the Baby Gem leaves, then top with the mozzarella mixture and some almond halves.

SWEETISH CARROT, MANGO, CORIANDER AND CURRY LEAF SALAD IN RICE PAPER WRAPPERS WITH CHILLIED VINEGAR

This salad is also delicious served under grilled fish or with poached or steamed chicken. Curry leaves are from India and have an almost nutty taste when deep-fried. Rice paper wrappers are from Vietnam and they come in assorted sizes and shapes – either as rounds or as quarter-rounds. I use 15cm diameter rounds here.

Place the orange and lemon juices in a small pot with the sugar and bring to the boil, then turn down to a simmer and reduce to 2 tablespoons.

Pour half of the reduction over the grated carrot in a large bowl and mix well, then pour the other half into a small dipping bowl. Add the vinegar and chilli to the dipping bowl and stir them in, then leave to one side.

Heat enough (a minimum of 3cm deep) oil in a small pan or a deep-fryer to 160°C and cook the curry leaves until crisp and golden – too brown and they'll taste bitter. Remove with a slotted spoon or spider and drain on kitchen paper.

Peel the mango, cut the flesh into 1 cm dice and add to the carrot mixture together with the coriander, chopped into 2 cm lengths, and the deep-fried curry leaves. Season with salt.

Fill a bowl, larger than the rice paper wrappers, with warm water. Lay a tea towel beside the bowl. One by one, submerge the wrappers in the bowl of water and count to 10, then place on the tea towel. Take one-tenth of the filling and place it firmly in the centre of the wrapper, in a sausage shape about 6cm long going from left to right. As soon as the wrapper is pliable, fold the end nearest you over the filling, keeping it as tight as possible, and roll it up halfway. Fold both the left and right sides into the centre, again keeping it tight, and finish rolling it up. Place seam-side down on a plate lined with cling film and finish rolling the rest. They may stick to each other so keep them slightly separated.

To serve, place the rolls on a platter with the bowl of chilli vinegar in the centre.

---

makes 8

juice of 1 orange and 1 lemon

2 tablespoons grated pale palm sugar or caster sugar

1 large carrot (200g), peeled and grated

100ml rice or cider vinegar

1 small mild chilli, finely chopped

vegetable oil for deep-frying

small handful of curry leaves, stems removed

1 large ripe (but not too soft) mango

handful of coriander stems with leaves

salt

8 rice paper wrappers (see above)

Vegetable Salads

that make the most
of a wide range of
vegetables and pulses

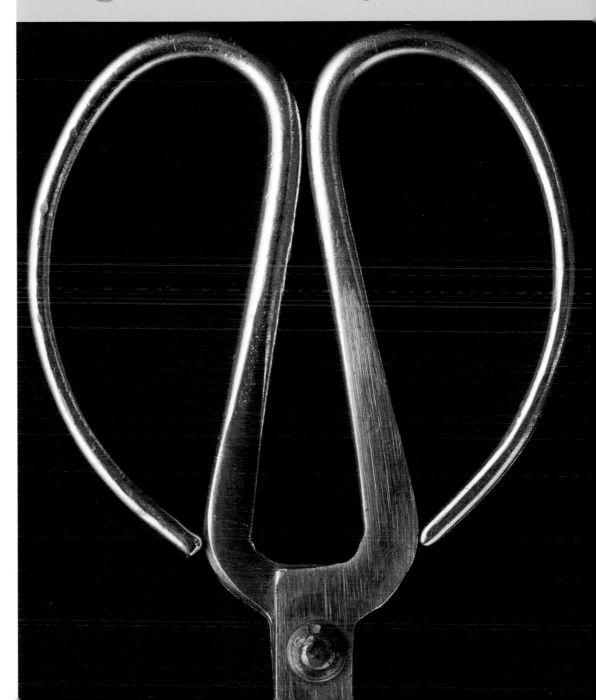

ISRAELI COUSCOUS, HIJIKI, RED ONION, TOMATO AND PARSLEY SALAD
WITH SPICY FRIED TOFU AND MINTED AUBERGINE SALAD

Israeli couscous is actually a type of 'pasta' made from wheat. The key to making it delicious is toasting it before cooking in the same way that you cook risotto, by the absorption method. If you're making this for a large number of people, you may prefer to toast the couscous in the oven.

Hijiki is just one of the fabulous family of edible seaweed – it is jet-black and comes in dried form from Japanese and health food shops. If you can't locate any, try arame - another more readily available seaweed.

Tofu – the ingredient that most chefs (macrobiotics aside) despise – is a really delicious ingredient. It lends itself to other flavours and provides an interesting texture to many dishes. Fresh tofu is called silken tofu, but you can also find firm and soft tofu vacuum-packed at most health food stores – and the difference is that one is firmer than the other. For frying purposes, use the firm type. Here the tofu is flavoured with a Japanese spice mixture that you'll also be able to source from Japanese food stores.

4 tablespoons extra-virgin olive oil

1 (250ml) cup of Israeli couscous (see above)

1 large red onion, thinly sliced

6 garlic cloves, sliced

4 tablespoons dried hijiki (see above)

500ml hot water

salt and freshly ground black pepper

6 best-quality ripe tomatoes

large handful of flat-leaf parsley

4 spring onions, sliced

250g firm tofu

2 tablespoons flour

1 teaspoon paprika

1 teaspoon coarsely ground fennel seeds

vegetable oil for frying

1 large aubergine, stem removed and cut into 2cm dice

4 limes

12 large mint leaves

200g fine green beans, blanched and refreshed in iced water

handful of sprouts (see page 16) for garnish

Heat a saucepan and add 3 tablespoons of the oil. Add the couscous and fry over a moderate heat for 4–5 minutes to colour to a dark golden, stirring frequently to prevent the grains from burning. Once they've coloured, tip them into a bowl.

Place the remaining olive oil in the pan and, when it's hot, add the onion. Cook over a moderate heat to caramelize, stirring frequently. Then add the garlic and hijiki, and cook for a further minute, stirring.

Return the couscous to the pan, pour in the hot water and $\frac{1}{2}$ teaspoon of salt, and bring to the boil. Boil for exactly 6 minutes, cover, take off the heat and leave to cool.

Cut the tomatoes into wedges and mix into the couscous with the parsley and spring onions, then taste and season.

Slice the tofu into cubes 1.5cm thick and lay them on a double thickness of kitchen paper to absorb excess water (and there will be a fair bit). Lay more paper on top and gently press down with your hands. Leave for 10 minutes, replacing the paper if you need to. Mix the flour with the paprika and ground fennel and gently toss the drained tofu in it, then shake between your fingers to remove excess flour. Fill a deep-fryer or pan with at least 5cm of oil and heat to 180°C. Fry the tofu in small batches until it turns golden, then drain on kitchen paper.

Cook the aubergine in several batches in the same oil and, when it's golden, remove and drain.

Grate 1 teaspoon of zest from one of the limes, then juice it and 1 other lime, and cut the other 2 in half to give you 4 wedges.

Once the tofu and aubergine have cooled to body temperature, toss with the mint leaves and lime zest and juice, and season lightly with salt.

To serve, divide the couscous salad between 4 plates or bowls and scatter the beans on top, then divide the tofu salad on top and finish with the sprouts and a lime wedge on the side.

BABY POTATO, GREEN BEAN, SPINACH AND RED ONION SALAD WITH LEMON DRESSING

600g baby or new potatoes (try something waxy like Kipfler, Anya or Pink Fir)

1 teaspoon salt

300g green beans, topped (I never remove the tails)

3 medium red onions, peeled

100ml extra-virgin olive oil

3 tablespoons balsamic vinegar

500g small spinach leaves

3 medium juicy lemons

handful of sprouts (see page 16) or cress

This is the sort of lunch I love to eat on a hot summer's day, followed by fresh fruit as dessert. The use of the spinach and red onion in two different ways gives added texture to the dish.

Put the potatoes into a generously sized pot, cover with cold water, add the teaspoon of salt and boil until just cooked. As soon as they're cooked, add the beans to the same pan (making sure there is enough water to cover them) and cook for a further 2 minutes. Drain in a colander and refresh under cold running water for a few minutes.

Meanwhile, halve 2 of the onions, thinly slice them and sauté in half the olive oil in a large pan until caramelized, stirring them every now and then.

Once the onions are ready, add the balsamic vinegar and cook to evaporate it off. Add two-thirds of the spinach to the same pan and cook it gently to wilt down. Tip the mixture on to a plate and put to one side to cool down.

Slice the remaining onion finely into rings (a mandolin grater is a good piece of equipment for doing this). Place in a colander sitting in a bowl and gently run cold water through it for 5 minutes to crisp the onion up and remove some of its raw flavour.

To make the dressing, finely grate 1/2 teaspoon of lemon zest from 1 of the lemons, then juice the lemon too. Add the remaining olive oil to the juice, lightly season and mix together.

Segment the remaining lemons. Cut off their tops and bottoms. Stand them on a cut side on a board and, using a small sharp knife, cut the skin and rind off in downward slices. What you want to end up with is what looks like a peeled lemon with no pith attached, but you also need to make sure you haven't removed too much flesh. Now hold the lemon in your hand over the bowl of dressing to collect the juices and carefully remove the segments by slicing into the centre of the lemon, cutting close to the membrane that separates each segment. Once you've removed all segments, squeeze any juice from the core into the dressing. Remove the pips from the segments.

To serve, divide the cooked spinach mixture between 4 plates. Either serve the potatoes whole if they're small enough, or slice them. Toss the potatoes with the beans, the raw spinach, half the red onion rings and half the dressing, then sit this on top of the spinach mixture. Scatter the lemon segments and remaining onion rings on top and finally drizzle over the remaining dressing and scatter over the sprouts or cress.

GREEN TEA OR SOBA NOODLE SALAD WITH FRIED TOFU, MUSHROOMS, SMOKED PAPRIKA, CUMIN ALMONDS, PAK CHOY, WASABI MIRIN DRESSING

Green tea and soba noodles are nutty firm noodles from Japan. The former are made from wheat with added powdered green tea, and the latter can be either a mixture of wheat and buckwheat or 100 per cent buckwheat. I prefer the mixed-grain soba noodle, as the pure buckwheat noodle can be quite brittle and almost crunchy.

The tofu here is the same type and cooked in much the same way as in the recipe on page 34. Mirin is Japanese rice wine used only for cooking and is nowadays widely available in better supermarkets.

Preheat the oven to 170°C, gas 3½ and line a baking tray with baking parchment. Mix the almonds with the pimenton, icing sugar, cumin and sesame seeds, and 1 teaspoon of the sesame oil. Lay on the lined baking tray and bake until golden, 10–15 minutes, tossing from time to time as they cook. Tip out on to a plate and leave to cool, then roughly chop.

Bring a very large pot half-filled with lightly salted water to the boil. Add the noodles and, after 30 seconds, give them a stir. Bring back to the boil, then add a cupful of cold water to 'shock' the noodles, and cook until al dente. Drain in a colander and refresh under cold running water and drain again. The reason you need to use a large pot is that these noodles often 'foam up' and boil over.

Slice the tofu into pieces 1.5cm thick and lay on a double thickness of kitchen paper to absorb excess water (and there will be a fair bit). Press more paper on top and gently press down with your hands. Leave for 10 minutes, replacing the paper if you need to. Gently coat the slices all over with the flour. Heat a frying pan and add a few millimetres of oil, then cook the tofu on both sides to colour it golden. Remove to a plate.

Depending on your mushrooms, you can either keep them whole or slice them if they're large. Heat a little more cooking oil with the remaining sesame oil and sauté the mushrooms to soften them. Then add the soy sauce and take off the heat – you want them still to have a little bite.

Blanch the pak choy by plunging it into boiling water for 30 seconds, then drain and refresh.

Make the wasabi mirin dressing, whisk the wasabi paste into the vinegar and mirin, then whisk in the oil and season it.

To serve, mix the noodles with a little of the dressing and divide between 4 plates. Toss the mushrooms with the pak choy and sit this on top, then place pieces of the tofu on that, drizzle the remaining dressing over, then sprinkle over the almonds and spring onions.

100g blanched almonds

1 teaspoon pimenton (smoked paprika, either dulce or picante – you choose)

1 teaspoon icing sugar

1 teaspoon cumin seeds

1 teaspoon sesame seeds

2 teaspoons roasted sesame oil

salt

150g noodles (dry weight, see above)

200g firm tofu

2 tablespoons flour

vegetable oil for frying

300g mushrooms (any type or a mixture)

2 tablespoons soy sauce

400g pak choy (bok choy), leaves separated

2 spring onions, thinly sliced and rinsed under cold running water for 2 minutes

for the wasabi mirin dressing

1 teaspoon (or more or less to taste) wasabi paste

2 tablespoons rice wine vinegar

2 tablespoons mirin

3 tablespoons light salad oil (grapeseed, light olive or sunflower)

salt and freshly ground black pepper

WARM SEVEN MUSHROOM SALAD WITH HOISIN AND GINGER DRESSING

I call this autumnal brunch meal 'Seven Mushroom Salad' for the very obvious reason that it uses seven types of mushroom, but don't let this dictate the meal. If you can only get three or four varieties, then just use more of each of them – and if you can get a larger variety, then go for it. I like to serve this on grilled sourdough – a play on mushrooms on toast. A good dollop of mascarpone or ricotta put on the toast first is also delicious and works surprisingly well with the ginger and sesame oil.

Heat half the butter in a pan and add the chestnut mushrooms, garlic and thyme. Sauté over moderate heat, shaking the pan occasionally. After 2 minutes, add the soy sauce and balsamic vinegar. Cook to reduce the liquids by half, then tip the mushrooms and juices into a bowl. You can eat these mushrooms raw, so don't worry that you've undercooked them.

Put the pan back on the heat and add the olive oil, then add the pied bleu, pied de mouton and shimeji mushrooms. Cook over a moderate-to-high heat and toss often until the mushrooms have softened a little but kept their shape. Tip the mushrooms into another bowl and keep warm.

Put the remaining butter and the sesame oil in the pan (don't wipe it out first) and bring to a sizzle. Add the ginger and count to 10, then add the chanterelles and trompettes, and sauté until they begin to wilt. Stir in the hoisin sauce and put to one side.

To serve, place 2 slices of toast on each of 4 plates and lay the chestnut mushrooms on top with their juices. Spoon over the mushrooms cooked in the olive oil, followed by the mushrooms cooked in the sesame oil. Lastly scatter the enoki over the top and eat while warm.

120g butter

200g chestnut mushrooms

1 garlic clove, chopped

8 stalks of fresh thyme

2 tablespoons light soy sauce (if you're using the thick Chinese soy, then half this amount)

2 tablespoons balsamic vinegar

4 tablespoons extra-virgin olive oil

150g pied bleu (wood blewit) mushrooms

150g pied de mouton (wood hedgehog) mushrooms

150g shimeji mushrooms

2 tablespoons sesame oil

2 teaspoons finely julienned or grated fresh ginger (or use finely shredded sushi pickled ginger)

100g chanterelles (girolles)

100g trompettes des morts (horns of plenty)

3 tablespoons hoisin sauce

8 slices of sourdough bread, toasted

100g enoki mushrooms

Just remember that wild mushrooms are exactly that... WILD. So chances are they'll have bracken, twigs, leaves and the like among them. The best way to clean them is to do it one by one. Remove the twigs, brush the grit off with a pastry brush and scrape off the dirt. Try to avoid washing them unless absolutely necessary, as they absorb water and the flavour is diluted – although sometimes it's the only way. No wonder restaurants charge so much for them – the labour involved is sometimes scary! I like to cook this in a pan with a tight-fitting lid – that way the mushrooms cook but don't ever dry out as they do so.

SALAD OF ASPARAGUS WITH ARTICHOKES, PURSLANE, POMEGRANATE AND BEETROOT WITH WHITE BALSAMIC DRESSING

This is an early summer salad that makes a great lunch main course after a starter of smoked salmon and rye toast. If you're making this at the start of summer, then try it with sea kale – a delicious vegetable from coastal regions, particularly in Scotland.

White balsamic vinegar is a relatively new food product; it isn't exactly white or clear in colour, but it is very pale. With much less of a caramel flavour than regular balsamic, it's a good vinegar to have in the pantry.

I have used purslane and nasturtium leaves in my salads, which I know aren't going to be available everywhere – if necessary just substitute some good leaves that taste great and look even better. I also use striped beetroot, but regular red beets will be just as tasty.

300g medium-sized striped beetroot

2 tablespoons cider vinegar

1 teaspoon salt

2 tablespoons white balsamic vinegar

4 large artichokes

1 lemon, sliced into 1cm rounds

1 large pomegranate

400g asparagus spears

100g purslane

small handful of nasturtium leaves

3 tablespoons extra-virgin olive oil

Place the beetroot in a pot with the cider vinegar and the teaspoon of salt. Cover with cold water, bring to the boil, cover and cook for 30–40 minutes. They're ready when you can insert a thin sharp knife into their centres. Leave to cool in the liquid, then remove and peel by rubbing the skin off with your fingers, or use a peeler or sharp knife if they're stubborn. (It's advisable to wear gloves for this, as otherwise the beetroot will stain your hands.) Slice really thinly with a mandolin grater or sharp knife and mix with the white balsamic vinegar.

Hold the artichokes horizontally by their stem and slice down through the leaves leaving about 3cm of the head. Cut off the stem and trim away the outer leaves with a sharp paring knife. Then you need to scrape the feathery centre, or choke, out with a teaspoon – just dig it in and scoop it out – revealing the inner heart or 'fond'. Rinse well under cold running water and place in a pot with 1 litre of cold water and the sliced lemon. The artichokes discolour quickly, so do all this as you prepare each one. Once they're all done, bring to the boil, then cook at a rapid simmer until you can insert a knife into the thickest part of the heart. Drain, run cold water over them for a minute, then leave to cool and slice into pieces 1cm thick.

Run a sharp knife around the outside off the pomegranate just cutting the skin, then twisting it very hard to break it in half. This avoids cutting into the sour body and fibres, which will taint the seeds. Turn the halves inside out by pushing hard with your thumb, then break the seeds away from the body. Do this over a bowl as the juice will dribble out and you don't want to stain your clothes. Once all the seeds and juice are removed, make sure no pith is attached, and put to one side.

Bring a pot of salted water to the boil and add the asparagus. Boil for 1–2 minutes depending on size, drain and refresh in iced water, then drain again.

To serve, arrange some asparagus on a plate and place the artichoke slices on top. Scatter over the purslane and then sit the beetroot on that. Scatter over the pomegranate seeds and their juice, place the nasturtium leaves on top, then drizzle with the vinegar from the beetroot and the olive oil.

WARM PEA, BROAD BEAN, FENNEL AND HERB ROASTED SWEET POTATO SALAD WITH PARMESAN DRESSING

Sweet potato and Parmesan seem, to me at least, a match made in culinary heaven. Definitely 'fusion food' when put together (Italians aren't known for using sweet potato), they carry each other – and each other's flavours -– so well. Fresh peas are one of summer's highlights (along with swimming in a river and eating a fresh mango in the sea), but if you can't get fresh peas then don't feel bad about using frozen ones – often they'll be frozen within hours of being picked, so buy a good brand and just don't tell your guests!

Preheat the oven to 200°C, gas 6. Line a wide roasting dish with baking parchment and add the sweet potato, garlic, 2 tablespoons of the olive oil and the herbs, and mix together. Add 4 tablespoons of water to the dish and roast for 20–30 minutes, until the potato is just cooked, tossing twice as it bakes. (The water stops the potato sticking to the paper, and the paper in turn stops the whole lot from sticking to the dish.)

Meanwhile, using a mandolin grater or a sharp knife, slice the fennel into very thin rounds. If the broad beans are large, remove their grey skin by tearing it and squeezing the green centres out; but if the beans are small and sweet, then don't bother.

In a large bowl, mix the remaining olive oil with half the Parmesan and all of the lemon juice, then add a little salt and pepper and mix in the broad beans, peas and fennel.

Once the potato is cooked, sprinkle the remaining Parmesan over it and toss together, then divide this between 4 warmed plates. Lay the salad greens on top, then add the fennel salad last of all.

800g sweet potato, peeled and cut into 2cm chunks

1 garlic clove, thinly sliced

5 tablespoons extra-virgin olive oil

generous handful of fresh herbs (use either rosemary, thyme or oregano, or a mixture of all three)

2 medium-sized heads of fennel

700g fresh broad beans, podded (podded weight about 250g), cooked until tender and refreshed in iced water

4 large tablespoons finely grated Parmesan

4 tablespoons fresh lemon juice

salt and freshly ground black pepper

500g fresh peas, podded (podded weight about 200g), cooked until tender and refreshed in iced water

large handful of salad greens (I used amaranth, but choose whatever adds colour and flavour – try shredded radicchio or red chicory, rocket or dandelion)

COURGETTE, FENNEL, APPLE, HAZELNUT AND ASPARAGUS SALAD
WITH LOTS OF GREENS, APPLE BALSAMIC DRESSING

This is one of those salads that are great all tumbled together, packed with lots of different leaves and fresh crunchy vegetables. It makes the perfect summer lunch salad with a crisp baguette.

First make the apple balsamic dressing, place the apple juice and balsamic vinegar in a small pan and cook to reduce to about one-quarter of its volume. Season with salt and pepper, then leave to cool. Mix in the olive oil.

Using a potato peeler, peel ribbons from the courgettes, discarding the soft seedy part in the centre. Thinly slice the fennel into 'rings' (a mandolin grater is ideal for this). Cut the asparagus spears at an angle into short lengths. Cut the hazelnuts in half or roughly chop them.

Divide half the greens between 4 plates and place the remainder in a large bowl. Quarter the apples and remove the core (you can also peel them if you want), then thinly slice them and add to the bowl with all the remaining ingredients, including two-thirds of the dressing. Toss well together and divide between the 4 plates. Drizzle the remaining dressing over and serve immediately.

4 medium courgettes

3 heads of fennel

24 asparagus spears, trimmed and blanched, then refreshed in iced water

2 handfuls of toasted hazelnuts, skins removed

2 large handfuls of assorted greens (watercress, rocket, chicory, Cos etc.)

4 apples (I like to use 2 Granny Smiths and 2 Red Delicious)

handful of sprouts (see page 16) for garnish

for the apple balsamic dressing

250ml apple juice

6 tablespoons balsamic vinegar

salt and freshly ground black pepper

125ml extra-virgin olive oil

PUY LENTIL, AVOCADO, GREEN BEAN, BABY GEM AND RED ONION SALAD, POMEGRANATE MOLASSES AND AVOCADO OIL DRESSING

It wasn't until the Puy lentil hit restaurant menus just over 14 years ago that these 'hippie grains' became fashionable. For years they'd been dismissed as being too homely and too worthy. In this case it's a good thing that 'fashion' stepped in. Lentils offer a really earthy flavour and texture, and they are truly delicious when cooked properly.

New Zealand has led the way in avocado oil production in recent years, and it's well worth sourcing it for a variety of culinary applications – here it works wonders as a dressing alongside the fresh avocado.

1 (250ml) cup of Puy lentils

2 medium red onions

4 tablespoons extra-virgin olive oil

2 garlic cloves, sliced

1 tablespoon fresh rosemary leaves, roughly chopped

10 fresh sage leaves, sliced

2 teaspoons fresh thyme leaves

salt and freshly ground black pepper

2 tablespoons vinegar (rice, white wine and cider vinegars are all good)

2 ripe avocados

2 large handfuls of green beans, blanched and refreshed in iced water

3 Baby Gem lettuces, leaves separated

for the pomegranate molasses and avocado oil dressing

3 tablespoons pomegranate molasses

3 tablespoons avocado oil

3 tablespoons extra-virgin olive oil

Rinse the lentils and drain. Halve 1 of the onions, thinly slice it and sauté in the olive oil with the garlic until caramelized. Add the herbs and sauté for a further 2 minutes, then add the lentils with 700ml water and bring to the boil. Cover and simmer until just cooked, about 30-40 minutes. Make sure they don't dry out and, if they need it, add a little extra boiling water from time to time until they're cooked (rather than adding too much in one go and having to drain them at the end and lose lots of flavour). Once cooked, season and leave to cool completely. You can store, covered, in the fridge for up to 4 days.

Slice the remaining onion thinly into rings and mix with the vinegar, which will make it go a lovely pinky-red colour.

Make the pomegranate molasses and avocado oil dressing by whisking the ingredients together, then lightly season.

Split the avocados in half, remove the stones, peel off the skin and cut the flesh into chunks.

To serve, put the lentils into a bowl with the avocado, beans, Baby Gem, half the onion and its vinegar, and the dressing. Toss everything together and then divide between 4 plates. Scatter over the remaining onion. This salad is also lovely served topped with a big dollop of thick plain yoghurt.

ASPARAGUS, BABY POTATO, ROCKET, BASIL AND WATERCRESS SALAD WITH ROAST OLIVES, SULTANAS AND CHERRY TOMATOES

600g cherry tomatoes

4 tablespoons extra-virgin olive oil

2 handfuls of plump olives, any type

2 small handfuls of sultanas

1 tablespoon fresh oregano leaves

2 tablespoons soy sauce

2 tablespoons cider vinegar

500g baby potatoes

salt

600g asparagus

large handful of rocket

large handful of watercress

large handful of basil leaves, roughly torn

It's the contrast of the tangy cherry tomatoes and sweet sultanas that lifts this salad into a tasty meal, almost more than the sum of its parts. I like just to toss it all together and let people help themselves – it's a very casual meal that's best followed by a bowl of fruit and ice cream.

Preheat the oven to 180°C, gas 4. Place the tomatoes in a large deep square non-reactive roasting dish.

Place the olive oil in a pan with the olives and cook over a moderate heat to blister them slightly, then add them to the tomatoes in the roasting dish, leaving the oil in the pan.

Add the sultanas to the pan and cook them – they will puff up a little, but make sure you don't burn them. Add the oregano to the pan and stir in, then add the soy sauce and vinegar, and bring to the boil. Pour over the tomatoes and olives.

Bake in the oven until the first few tomatoes are just beginning to pop open. Take from the oven and leave to go cold. They can then be stored in the fridge for up to 3 days.

Cook the potatoes in plenty of salted water until tender, then refresh in cold water and leave to cool. Steam or boil the asparagus until just tender and refresh in iced water, then snap the ends off. To do this, hold both ends of the asparagus 3–4cm from both ends and bend in half. It will snap at the point that the stem becomes tough – anything below the snap can be discarded, the tip will be tender. Cut the potatoes into small wedges and cut the asparagus at an angle into 5cm lengths.

To serve, place the rocket, watercress and basil in a large bowl with the potatoes and asparagus, and toss everything together. Spoon the tomato, olive and sultana mixture on top and get your guests to help themselves.

Cheese Salads

built around cheeses of all types, fresh and aged, soft and hard

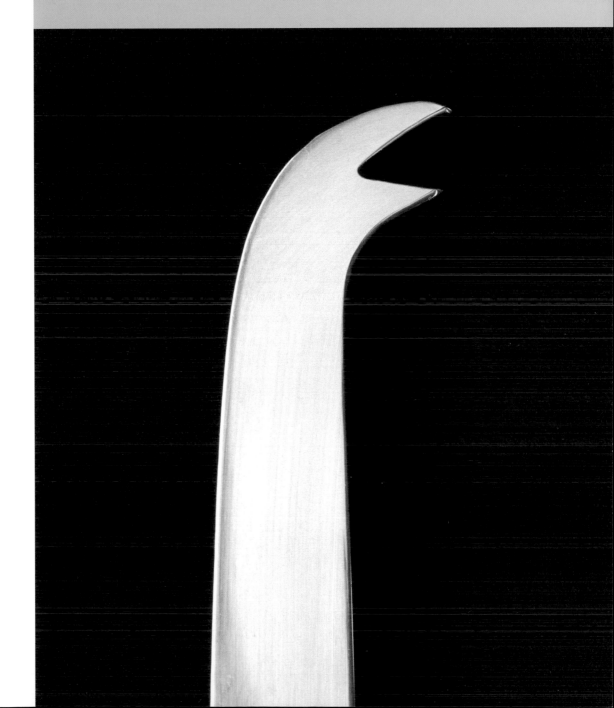

TWEAKED TRICOLORE
PAN-BURST CHERRY TOMATO AND MOZZARELLA SALAD WITH GUACAMOLE, BASIL OIL AND CORN CHIPS

1 tablespoon extra-virgin olive oil

2 handfuls of cherry tomatoes

600g mozzarella, at room temperature, cut into chunks.

400g best-quality corn chips

for the basil dressing
handful of basil leaves

2 tablespoons avocado oil

salt

for the guacamole
3 ripe avocados

2 tablespoons avocado oil

2 tablespoons fresh lime juice

1 mild red chilli, thinly sliced (more or less to taste)

handful of coriander, roughly chopped

2 spring onions, thinly sliced

The tricolore salad is one of cuisine's mysteries – to me at least. It seems so odd that this classic salad is a staple in most London Italian cafés, yet avocado and mozzarella must be one of the oddest combinations - hardly one that you can imagine the great Italian chefs of the past encouraging. However, it's one that works, even if I can't quite get my head around it. And for me, a devoted exponent to fusion cuisine, that's saying something.

Heat a wide pan over a high heat until smoking, then add the olive oil and the tomatoes, and leave for 30 seconds. Gently shake the pan and cook for another 2 minutes, until some of the skins begin to colour and a few of the tomatoes burst. Take off the heat and leave to cool in the pan.

Make the basil dressing, finely chiffonade (shred) the basil leaves and put into a jar with half the avocado oil and 2 pinches of salt. Shake well and leave in a warm place, in sunlight if possible, for 10 minutes.

Make the guacamole, cut the avocados in half, remove the stones and peel them. The best way is to scoop out the flesh with a large dessertspoon. Place the flesh in a bowl and add the remaining ingredients. Then roughly mash with a fork or potato masher, season and mix again.

To serve: place a large dollop of the guacamole on 4 plates, place one-quarter of the mozzarella chunks next to it and then spoon the tomatoes and their juices on the other side. Drizzle the basil dressing over everything, then tuck the corn chips into the guacamole.

SALAD OF CRUMBED CHÈVRE, CHERRY TOMATOES, GREEN BEANS, PEAS AND DANDELION WITH APPLE AND GINGER DRESSING

A log of chèvre – a French cheese made from goats' milk – is a lovely cheese to crumb and serve warm. It can have a dry texture, but softens up when heated and has an inherent acidity that goes well with sweet tomatoes and peas. The ginger in the dressing isn't at all a traditional combination (so few of mine are), but its aromatic qualities really highlight and contrast with the chèvre. If you're able to source the Japanese breadcrumbs called panko then try them – they have a fantastic texture – but regular crumbs will work just as well.

Season the flour with a little salt and pepper and toss the chèvre pieces in it. Dip the chèvre in the beaten egg to coat, then roll in the crumbs to cover completely, pressing in well to make stick. Place in the fridge until needed.

Make the apple and ginger dressing, you can peel the apple if you want, though I don't bother, then remove the core and chop into small dice, about 5mm square. Place in a small pan with the ginger and apple juice or cider, and bring to a boil, then simmer and reduce by two-thirds. Add the vinegar and taste: if it's too sour, add a little honey, maple syrup or sugar. Leave the dressing to cool.

Cut the tomatoes in half and mix with the olive or avocado oil and a little salt and pepper.

Heat a pan large enough to hold the chèvre in one layer and, when it's just beginning to smoke, add a few tablespoons of vegetable oil and place the chèvre in the pan. Cook until golden on one side, then flip over and cook until golden on the other side. If the chèvre is very thick, you can also cook the sides by slowly rolling them in the pan on their side to colour before cooking their top and bottom.

To serve, toss the tomatoes, beans, peas and dandelion leaves together with half the apple dressing and divide between 4 plates. Sit a piece of warm chèvre on top, then drizzle over the remaining dressing.

2 tablespoons flour

salt and freshly ground black pepper

4 slices of chèvre, each about 150g (or 8 of 75g), straight from the fridge

1 egg, lightly beaten

breadcrumbs, for coating

3 handfuls of cherry tomatoes

1 tablespoon extra-virgin olive oil or avocado oil

vegetable oil for frying

2 large handfuls of green beans, blanched and refreshed in iced water

2 large handfuls of green peas, blanched and refreshed in iced water

2 handfuls of dandelion leaves (or any slightly bitter leaves, such as escarole, frisée, curly endive or even trevissano)

for the apple and ginger dressing

1 tart apple, such as a Granny Smith

1 finger of peeled ginger, finely julienned or grated

240ml apple juice or apple cider

1 tablespoon cider vinegar

a little honey, maple syrup or sugar to taste (optional)

YELLOW COURGETTE, CHICKPEA, RED ONION, CHILLI, WATERCRESS AND FETA SALAD, BASIL CRÈME FRAÎCHE DRESSING

5 tablespoons extra-virgin olive oil

3 large red onions, thinly sliced

4 garlic cloves, thinly sliced

1 moderately hot red chilli, thinly sliced into rings (remove the seeds if you want less heat)

2 teaspoons fresh thyme leaves

4 tablespoons fresh lemon juice and 1 teaspoon grated lemon zest

600g cooked chickpeas, drained and rinsed if from a can

handful of picked flat leaf parsley

250g feta, cut into small chunks

4 medium yellow courgettes, topped and tailed

salt

2 handfuls of watercress

for the basil and crème fraîche dressing

1 cup loosely packed basil leaves

½ teaspoon sugar

3 tablespoons crème fraîche

Yellow courgettes are a very pretty vegetable; they have a lovely colour and seem to brighten up a plate of food fairly easily. If you can't find any, just use ordinary green ones, but make sure they're very fresh.

I tend always to cook chickpeas from scratch as I like to buy those lovely tiny Spanish ones, but if you aren't sure how old your dried chickpeas are I'd recommend you buy a good-quality canned variety. It will save you hours in preparation and cooking time.

I use a lot of olive oil to make this as the oil forms part of the dressing, but if you're on a low-oil diet, then use a non-stick pan to cook the onions and cut back – but it won't be quite as delicious! This is great served at room temperature – never straight from the fridge if prepared in advance.

Heat all but 1 tablespoon of the oil in a wide pan and cook the onions to wilt them, about 5 minutes, stirring occasionally. Add the garlic, chilli and thyme, and continue to cook until the onions are caramelized. Add the lemon juice and zest, and the chickpeas, and cook for another 4 minutes, stirring frequently to make sure it doesn't catch on the bottom. Take off the heat and tip into a bowl. When it has cooled a little, mix in the parsley and feta, and leave to one side.

To make the basil and crème fraîche dressing: place the basil and sugar in a mortar and grind to a paste with a pestle, then mix in the crème fraîche and 1 tablespoon of cold water and lightly season. Alternatively, finely chiffonade (shred) the basil and mix with the sugar, crème fraîche, water and seasoning.

Peel the courgettes into ribbons with a potato peeler. Peel one side until you get to the centre, then peel the opposite side. Lastly peel the sides off. You want every piece to have some of the yellow skin on it. Bring a pot of salted water to the boil and add the courgettes, gently stir, count to 20 and then drain and rinse under cold water and drain again.

To serve, arrange the courgette slices around the outside rim of your plates, and place the watercress on the inside. Divide the chickpea salad on top of the watercress. Serve the basil dressing to the side and let your guests help themselves.

KUMARA (SWEET POTATO), BAKED SPICED RICOTTA, SPINACH AND ROAST GRAPE SALAD WITH OLIVE AND CAPER DRESSING

Kumara are the native New Zealand sweet potato that were introduced by the first wave of Maori, arriving from the Pacific island of Rarotonga over 500 years ago. They are dense and sweet, but earthily sweet in a savoury way – if that makes sense!

Ricotta comes in many degrees of quality. The best tend to have a grainy and slightly lumpy texture, but often all you'll be able to source is a very smooth type, which is fine for baking but not the best to eat raw.

400g ricotta

½ teaspoon sweet pimenton (smoked paprika), or use mild paprika

¼ teaspoon cumin seeds

¼ teaspoon ground cinnamon

2 tablespoons extra-virgin olive oil

sea salt and freshly ground black pepper

600g kumara or sweet potato, skins scrubbed

4 tablespoons hot water

300g grapes, off the stem

2 tablespoons pomegranate molasses

3 tablespoons grapeseed oil (or use a light vegetable or olive oil)

1 teaspoon soy sauce

2 handfuls of olives, stoned and roughly chopped

2 tablespoons baby capers, rinsed

12 mint leaves, shredded

2 tablespoons thinly sliced chives

400g baby spinach

Preheat the oven to 180°C, gas 4, and line a baking tray with baking parchment. Slice the ricotta into 2cm thick pieces and lay on the lined tray. Mix the pimenton, cumin and cinnamon together with 1 teaspoon of the olive oil and brush this on the cheese. Sprinkle lightly with sea salt and bake for 15 minutes, then take from the oven and leave to cool. Turn the oven up to 200°C, gas 6.

Cut the kumara into long thin wedges and place in a roasting dish, then pour in the hot water, season with salt and pepper and drizzle over the remaining olive oil. Bake until just cooked (you'll be able to insert a knife into them easily at the fattest end) and remove from oven.

Meanwhile, place the grapes into a non-reactive dish and pour on the pomegranate molasses, grapeseed oil and soy sauce. Bake this for 20 minutes in the same oven. Remove when done and leave to cool.

Once everything's at room temperature, pour the juice from the cooked grapes into a bowl and mix in the olives, capers, mint and chives to form the dressing.

To serve, toss the spinach with half the dressing and place on 4 plates. Scatter pieces of kumara on top, then flake the ricotta on top of that. Scatter over the grapes, then drizzle the remaining dressing over the lot.

Wild asparagus are a beautiful shade of green, with a lovely grassy asparagus taste. They arrive around May in the UK and if you have trouble finding them just use thin asparagus. The buffalo mozzarella I used for this dish was truly delicious – and truly expensive, as it was flown in from Napoli the day before. It was a taste experience that photographer Jean Cazals said he'd not had before but would like to repeat often. Tomatillos can be replaced with tomatoes, but chose ones that are slightly green to give a crunch.

First, cook the artichokes: place them in a pot just large enough to hold them in one layer – a deep 30cm frying pan is a good size. Smash 4 of the garlic cloves with the flat of a knife and tuck them in among the artichokes together with the thyme and bay leaf. Peel the rind from one of the lemons and juice it, then add both the peel and the juice to the pan with some salt. Add all but 2 tablespoons of the olive oil to the pan, then add enough water almost to cover the artichokes and bring to the boil. Place a paper cartouche, or suitably sized plate or saucer, over the artichokes to keep them submerged and turn the heat down to a rapid simmer, then continue to cook until you can just insert a skewer into the thickest part of one of the artichokes, about 15 minutes. Remove the cartouche, plate or saucer and simmer for 2 minutes more, then take off the heat and leave to cool. At this stage, they can be stored covered in the fridge for up to 5 days. (The marinating oil left over makes an excellent salad dressing.)

Peel the husk from the tomatillos and rinse them, then remove the core and cut into 1cm dice. Using a soup spoon, skim 2 spoonfuls of the artichoke braising oil and add to the tomatillos together with the juice of the remaining lemon and a little salt and freshly ground black pepper. Leave to 'cure' for 5 minutes, then finish the salsa by mixing in the mint.

Bring a pot of water to the boil and add the wild asparagus, bring back to the boil and cook for 45 seconds. Then drain and refresh in very cold water (add a few ice cubes).

Make the bruschetta by grilling the sourdough slices, then rubbing them with the remaining garlic and drizzling with the reserved oil.

To serve, place a bruschetta on a plate, then sit an artichoke on top. Scatter the wild asparagus around it together with the salad leaves and olives. Sit the mozzarella inside the artichoke, the broken side facing up, and spoon the salsa on top.

4 large globe artichokes, trimmed and prepared and placed in acidulated water as described on page 42

5 garlic cloves

handful of fresh thyme

1 bay leaf

2 lemons

a little salt and freshly ground black pepper

200ml extra-virgin olive oil

2 large tomatillos

small handful of mint, coarsely torn

300g wild asparagus, stalk end trimmed

4 thick slices of heavy sourdough or similar bread

handful of purslane or other interesting salad greens

large handful of olives (I used the crunchy unpasteurized petite Lucques Royal from Provence)

600g best-quality buffalo mozzarella (I used half of a 300g cheese per portion)

WARM SALAD OF GRILLED PEAR, ROAST SICHUAN PEPPER ALMONDS, BALSAMIC BRAISED RED ONIONS, MÂCHE, GORGONZOLA DRESSING

Pear and blue cheese is one of those classic combinations that just work. This salad takes that idea and gives it a bit more grunt – layering on a few more flavours and textures. This is a lovely autumnal meal, perhaps following on from a light vegetable broth and then finished with a warm fruit tart with crème fraîche.

3 medium red onions, sliced into 1cm thick rings

1 tablespoon fresh rosemary, oregano or thyme leaves

3 tablespoons balsamic vinegar

125ml extra-virgin olive oil

4 tablespoons boiling water

salt and freshly ground black pepper

2 handfuls of whole almonds, skin either off or on

½ teaspoon freshly ground Sichuan pepper, sieved

1 tablespoon caster sugar

150g Gorgonzola

4 large ripe pears (crisp ones will work best)

400g mâche

Preheat the oven to 220°C, gas 7. Mix the onion rings and herbs, and put into a non-reactive baking dish just large enough to hold them comfortably. Pour on the balsamic vinegar, all but 1 tablespoon of the olive oil and the boiling water. Lightly season and seal tightly with foil. Bake in the centre of the oven for 50 minutes, then check to see how they are. You want them to steam away in their sealed baking dish; they will wilt, soften and change colour. They need to have lost almost all of their texture and become tender. If they need some more time, reseal and bake for another 20 minutes. Leave to cool to room temperature, then drain in a small colander or sieve, reserving the juices.

Turn the oven down to 170°C, gas 3½, and line a baking tray with baking parchment. Mix the almonds with the remaining oil, Sichuan pepper, half the caster sugar and a little salt. Bake on the lined tray, tossing every 5 minutes, until golden, about 15–20 minutes. Remove from the oven and leave to cool.

Make the dressing by placing the reserved onion juices in a small pan with the Gorgonzola and warming gently, stirring as you do so, to melt the cheese into the dressing, keeping it barely warm.

Preheat the grill. Cut the pears into slices about 1cm thick, cutting out the seeds with a sharp knife, and lay on a lightly oiled foil-lined tray. Place under the grill and cook to caramelize, then turn the pear slices over, sprinkle the remaining sugar over them and cook to really caramelize them. Remove from the grill.

To serve: divide half the pear pieces between 4 plates, then sit the mâche on top. Lay the remaining pears on top of this, scatter over the almonds and onions, then pour the dressing over.

FRIED HALOUMI TOPPED WITH CHILLI, SPINACH, WATER CHESTNUT, HAZELNUT, ORANGE AND SUN-BLUSHED TOMATO SALAD

Haloumi is a very firm cheese found in Cyprus, Greece and Turkey, and it has a habit of making your teeth stand on edge if you eat a piece that's too thick – it's almost as though you're eating firm rubber! But, fear not, once you grill or fry it, it's delicious. My friends Tarik and Savas, who own changa restaurant in Istanbul, always soak slices of it in water before cooking it – which softens it and gives it a more mozzarella-like texture.

If you have problems sourcing water chestnuts, buy a reliable canned brand and rinse well in cold water for a few minutes before using. Sun-blushed tomatoes are juicier than sun-dried, and often much sweeter, as some producers sprinkle them with sugar before drying them.

Fill a bowl or roasting dish with 5cm warm water and place the haloumi slices in it in a single layer. Leave at room temperature for 2–6 hours, or overnight in the fridge.

Thinly slice the chilli into rings and place in a small pan with the garlic and half the olive oil. Bring to a gentle simmer and keep on the heat for 2 minutes – you don't want the garlic to colour too much, but you do need the flavours to infuse. Take off the heat, pour the contents into a small jug, then pour in the remaining oil and the vinegar and leave this dressing to one side.

Bring a large pot of water to the boil and put half the spinach in it. Press it down to submerge it, then count to 15. Immediately drain it into a colander and then refresh it in a large bowl of cold water. Squeeze out excess water. Shred the remaining spinach with a sharp knife.

Fill a 1 litre container with cold water, add the lemon juice and a teaspoon of salt, then mix to dissolve. Peel the water chestnuts with either a small sharp knife or a potato peeler and place in the acidulated water.

Take the haloumi from the soaking water and pat dry on kitchen paper. Heat a frying pan and add a few tablespoons of olive oil, then fry the haloumi slices until golden on both sides. Remove from the pan and place on 4 plates.

Take the blanched spinach and pull it apart to loosen it a little, then place in a bowl together with the shredded spinach, orange segments, hazelnuts and sun-blushed tomatoes. Slice the peeled water chestnuts into rounds about 5mm thick and add to the bowl. Stir the chilli dressing, then pour half over the spinach salad with some salt and toss it all together. Divide this between the 4 plates, then spoon over the remaining chilli dressing and scatter on the parsley leaves.

500g haloumi, cut into 1cm slices

1 red chilli (ideally you do want a little heat in this and I prefer it to be quite fiery)

1 garlic clove, finely chopped or crushed

6 tablespoons extra-virgin olive oil

2 tablespoons red wine vinegar

3 large handfuls of large-leaf spinach, stems removed if too woody

juice of 1 lemon

salt

20 fresh water chestnuts

olive oil for frying

2 oranges, segmented (see page 150)

small handful of hazelnuts, lightly toasted and skins rubbed off

150g sun-blushed tomatoes

2 handfuls of dill sprigs

SPICY POACHED QUINCE, BABY GEM, ROAST PECANS, FRESH RICOTTA AND EDAMAME SALAD WITH MULLED WINE DRESSING

Quinces mark the start of the end of summer, and their texture is firmer and less juicy than the stone fruit they follow. However, with slow gentle cooking they develop into a rich textural mouthful. Quinces are funny creatures, as they take an awfully long time to cook compared to a pear, yet they become very soft when cooked and then firm up when cooled.

This salad relies on contrast of textures for its appeal as much as on flavour, with the crunch from the nuts and edamame (fresh soy beans) contrasting with the grainy ricotta – so it's important you use the best available ricotta. Avoid the supermarket creamed style and source the slightly grainy type. For variation, try to find a ewes'- or goats'-milk type.

500ml red wine (use something lively with a little spice, such as a Shiraz, Pinotage or Pinot Noir)

150g unrefined sugar

juice of 1 lemon and pared rind of ½ of it

1 red chilli (moderate heat), halved

piece of cinnamon stick about 5cm long

4 allspice berries, crushed

2 quinces

sea salt flakes

300g edamame (see above) in the pod (fresh or frozen)

1 small red onion

3 tablespoons extra-virgin olive oil

3 baby Little Gem lettuces, leaves separated

40 pecans, around 1 cupful, toasted

250g best-quality ricotta

Place the wine, sugar, lemon rind, chilli and spices in a small pan large enough to hold the quinces. Peel the quinces and cut them in half. Using a small knife or melon-baller, remove the core and then cut each half in two and place in the pan. Add enough hot water to allow the quinces to float 2cm off the bottom and place a cartouche, or appropriate plate or saucer, on top to hold them under the surface. Bring to the boil, then reduce the heat to a simmer and cook for 1 hour. Keep an eye on them so as to ensure that the quinces remain covered with poaching liquid, topping up with boiling water as necessary. They are cooked when you can insert a knife into them easily. Leave to cool in the liquid and store, covered, in the fridge. If kept submerged, they will keep for up to 2 weeks.

Bring a large pan of salted water to the boil and add the edamame, still in their pods. If frozen, cook them for 4 minutes; if fresh, cook them for 3–4 (you'll need to check them after 3). Drain the edamame into a colander and then refresh in cold running water for 3 minutes (or plunge into a bowl of iced water). Once cold, pod them by squeezing them between your fingers. Thinly slice the red onion into rings (a mandolin grater is good for this) and rinse in gently running cold water for a minute, then place in iced water to firm up slightly and set aside.

To make the dressing, cut the quinces into wedges and mix 150ml of the poaching liquid with the olive oil and the lemon juice.

To serve, drain the onion slices and pat dry. Divide half the Baby Gem leaves between 4 plates and place the remaining leaves in a bowl with the quince, edamame, half the onion slices and the pecans. Pour over half the dressing and gently mix, then place this on top of the plated lettuce leaves. Dollop the ricotta on top, scatter with the remaining onion rings and a little salt, then drizzle with the remaining dressing.

FIG, ALMOND, MÂCHE, YELLOW TOMATO, LANCASHIRE CHEESE AND BEAN SALAD

A sweet ripe fig warmed by the sun is one of summer's great pleasures. I have such memories from holidays in Turkey, Spain and France – as well as Melbourne's very hot summers. A firm crumbly cheese is a perfect match for a fig – Lancashire is one such cheese, but you could also try a young Pecorino or Cheddar (though please don't make this with pre-sliced Cheddar of dubious origins as there is no textural benefit to the salad).

Mâche, also called lamb's lettuce, looks great in a salad and has a subtle sweet flavour; if you can't find any, then try baby spinach, purslane or baby oak leaf.

Lay the figs in a shallow plate, snip off the hard ends of the stems and cut crosses into their tops going halfway down their depth. Gently pull the four corners out to open them up. Stir the honey in the lemon juice to dissolve it and season with a little salt and pepper. Drizzle this over the figs and leave to macerate for 20 minutes.

To serve, scatter the mâche on 4 plates and lay the beans and tomato slices on top, then sprinkle liberally with salt and pepper. Sit a fig (or 2 small figs) on each plate. Scatter with the almonds and flake the cheese over. If the cheese is firm, use a potato peeler to shave off slices; if it's crumbly, then just slice pieces off with a sharp knife or crumble it over the salad. Drizzle the lemon-honey mixture left in the plate after macerating over the salad and then pour over the olive oil.

4 large or 8 smaller ripe figs

1 tablespoon runny honey (try lavender or thyme honey)

juice of 1 juicy lemon

salt and freshly ground black pepper

300g mixed green and yellow beans, blanched and refreshed in iced water

8 large yellow tomatoes, cut into 1cm slices

2 large handfuls of mâche

2 handfuls of almonds, salted and lightly toasted (I used pre-roasted Marcona almonds from Spain – one of my favourite snacks)

200g Lancashire cheese

4 tablespoons extra-virgin olive oil

Fish and Shellfish Salads featuring fish and seafood, raw or cooked, smoked or pickled

CRAYFISH, AVOCADO, GRAPEFRUIT AND GINGER SALAD WITH WILD ROCKET AND CHIVE DRESSING

Like lobster, crayfish are so luxurious that it's good to eat them only occasionally. However, I can well remember the times as a child that Dad would go cray fishing with his mates and come home from Ngawi (almost the southernmost point in New Zealand's North Island) with 20–30 crayfish. We'd all gorge ourselves stupid, then take a week's break from them as they are really quite a rich meat.

You can cook them yourself, or buy pre-cooked crays or lobsters, which will be easier – but you do need to make sure you're buying something that was ideally cooked that morning and not a week before. To cook a crayfish, see page 140. If you can't get a hold of crayfish or lobster, then use cooked prawns instead – allow about 180g cooked weight per person.

1 thumb-sized piece of very fresh and young ginger (if the skin is too dark and dry you'd be better using ready-pickled sushi ginger, also called gari, from Japanese shops)

2 tablespoons fresh lime juice (or use 3 tablespoons lemon juice)

2 tablespoons mirin (or use 2 tablespoons caster sugar)

salt and freshly ground black pepper

3 large grapefruit, segmented (see page 150), all juice reserved

3 avocados

large handful of wild rocket

4 crayfish or lobster, each about 400g, cooked and the flesh removed (see page 140)

for the chive dressing

2 tablespoons thinly sliced chives

2 tablespoons light olive oil

1 tablespoon avocado oil

Thinly slice the ginger using a mandolin grater or a very sharp knife, then cut the slices into fine julienne strips. Mix with the lime juice, mirin and two pinches of salt, and leave to cure for 10 minutes, when it will pinken a little and loose its raw edge.

Segment the grapefruit and add any juices that drip off them to the ginger. Place the segments in a small bowl. Cut the avocados in half, twist out the stone and scoop out the flesh in one piece with a large spoon, then cut it into fat wedges.

To make the chive dressing, mix the chives with the oils and season with a little black pepper.

To serve, divide the rocket and avocado between 4 plates and lay the crayfish meat on top, then scatter with the grapefruit segments and the ginger and its juices. Drizzle the chive dressing on last of all, mixing it as you do so.

IKA MATA: RAROTONGAN RAW FISH SALAD WITH COCONUT, PAPAYA AND CHILLI

In Rarotonga, one of the Cook Islands in the Pacific Ocean north of New Zealand, they have a dish called ika mata. This is basically raw fish marinated in coconut and citrus juice. However, here I team it with papaya and chilli, to give it a sweetish spicy note. This is a fantastic summer main-course meal, served with a crunchy green salad on the side. Use a firm white flaky fish, such as snapper, cod or sea bass. Funnily enough, even though Captain Cook is the reason for the Cook Islands' name, he never actually visited, sailing way past them.

800g fish fillets (see above), all bones, scales and skin removed

120ml lime juice or 150ml lemon juice

1 medium red onion, thinly sliced and briefly rinsed in cold water

sea salt (use this rather than rock salt)

1 medium ripe papaya (paw paw), around 400–500g, peeled, halved and seeds removed

1 red chilli, thinly sliced into rings (more or less to taste)

200ml coconut milk (make sure it's unsweetened)

4 spring onions, thinly sliced

large handful of picked coriander leaves

Cut the fish into chunks about 1cm thick and place in a non-reactive bowl. Add half the citrus juice, the red onion and ¼ teaspoon of salt, and gently mix it all together. Cover and leave to marinate in the fridge for 20 minutes.

After this time, drain off the excess liquid and discard. Cut the papaya flesh into chunks the same size as the fish. Add to the fish together with the remaining citrus juice, some more salt to taste, the chilli and coconut milk, and leave to marinate in the fridge for another 15 minutes.

After this time, mix in the spring onions and coriander, taste and adjust the seasoning, if necessary, and serve slightly chilled.

SQUID, ROAST BUTTERNUT SQUASH, PEANUT, LIME, CORIANDER AND CHILLI SALAD

Squid is an unusual 'fishy protein' in many ways. It looks so odd to start with, and the giant ones can grow so large that they attack sperm whales and, in turn, are the favoured meal of the same whale. Also, in order to keep it edible, it needs to be either cooked very briefly at a high heat or for a long time on a low heat. Cleaning squid is one of those lovely tactile kitchen jobs, but chances are you'll buy it ready-prepared from your fishmonger. What you are after is an assortment of the head, wings and tentacles, with all the membranes and guts removed. Bear in mind that a large squid will take a lot more cooking than a small squid and that it will be easier to cut a large squid into chunks before cooking it.

1 large butternut squash, around 700–800g

3 tablespoons groundnut (peanut) oil (or any other cooking oil)

2 tablespoon soy sauce

salt and freshly ground black pepper

750g squid (cleaned weight)

handful of greens (I used pea shoots)

small bunch of coriander, leaves picked and the stems cut into 3cm lengths

lime wedges, to serve (optional)

for the dressing

large handful of blanched and toasted peanuts

1 hot red chilli, with the seeds in, roughly chopped (more or less to taste)

2 garlic cloves

3–4 limes (you'll need 1 teaspoon fresh grated lime zest and 120ml lime juice)

2 pinches of salt

large thumb-sized piece of palm sugar (or use 2 tablespoons Demerara sugar)

2 teaspoons Thai fish sauce

Preheat the oven to 180°C, gas 4. Peel the butternut squash, split it in half lengthways and then scoop out the seeds and discard. Cut it into 2–3cm chunks and toss with the groundnut oil, soy sauce and some freshly ground pepper. Place in a roasting dish and add a few tablespoons hot water, then roast until cooked, tossing after 20 minutes. The squash is cooked when you can insert the tip of a knife easily into the flesh. Take from the oven and leave to cool.

While the squash cooks, bring a large pot of salted water to a rolling boil and blanch your squid. Place the thickest pieces in first (if it's a large squid, this will be the tentacles; if it's a small squid, start with the body) and count to 20, then add the thinner pieces and count to 30. Tip into a colander and let it drain. If your squid is very small, you'll only need to cook it for 30 seconds in total.

Ideally, make the dressing using a pestle and mortar, although a small food processor – or even a good knife – will work. Place the peanuts in the mortar and smash them a bit to break them up, then tip them into a small bowl. Don't bother cleaning the pestle and mortar, just add the chilli, garlic, lime zest, salt and sugar, and smash and grind together to a paste. Then stir in the fish sauce and lime juice. Taste and adjust the seasoning. Tip this dressing into a large bowl. Slice the squid fairly thinly and add it to the dressing with the half the peanuts and the coriander stems, then toss everything together.

To serve, place the butternut squash on 4 plates, top with the greens and then divide the squid on top of that, making sure you drizzle the dressing on evenly. Lastly, scatter over the remaining peanuts and the coriander leaves. If you want, serve a lime wedge on the side.

Hot-smoked salmon is quite different from regular smoked salmon in that it's cooked at the same time as being smoked by the heat generated from the smoking. Regular smoked salmon may take up to 36 hours to smoke, whereas hot-smoked can take as little as 15 minutes and it will have a more pronounced smokiness. Hot-smoked salmon has the texture of roast fish, rather than the pliable slices you may be more familiar with, and this makes it great for flaking into salads and pasta dishes. I give a technique for smoking salmon at the end of the recipe – but you may just prefer to buy it!

The chilli oil will make more than you need, so keep the remainder in your fridge for up to 6 months, then use it to spruce up grills and salads or even fried eggs for breakfast.

HOT-SMOKED SALMON, AVOCADO, ASPARAGUS, BORLOTTI BEAN AND CHERVIL SALAD WITH SWEET CHILLIED AVOCADO OIL

Put the beans and herbs into a large pot with ½ teaspoon of salt. Cover with plenty of cold water and bring to the boil, then turn to a simmer and cook for 20–30 minutes until the beans are tender. Leave them to cool in their cooking liquor.

Meanwhile, place the chillies and sugar in a mortar or very small blender and pound or process to make a paste, adding a little of the vinegar if it helps. Tip the paste and the remaining vinegar into a small pan and bring to a simmer, then cook until the vinegar has almost all evaporated – keep a keen eye on it. Pour in the oil and bring the oil up to body temperature, then take off the heat. Leave to cool, then decant into a 400ml jar or bottle.

Cut the avocados in half, twist out the stones and scoop out the flesh in one piece with a large spoon. Cut into cubes or wedges.

To serve, lay the asparagus spears and salad leaves on the plate. Place the avocado on top, then flake the salmon over. Drain the beans and scatter them and the chervil on top, squeeze over the lemon juice, season with flaked salt and freshly ground pepper, and then finally drizzle the oil over – or let your guests do it to taste.

500g hulled borlotti beans (you'll need about 1.5kg beans in the pod)

small handful of mixed favourite hard herbs (thyme, oregano, sage and rosemary are good)

flaked salt and freshly ground pepper

2 hot red chillies, roughly chopped

3 tablespoons coarsely grated palm sugar (or use demerara sugar)

2 tablespoons cider vinegar

350ml extra-virgin avocado oil (or use olive oil)

2 avocados

400g blanched asparagus spears, woody ends snapped off and discarded (see page 50)

2 large handfuls of salad leaves

600g hot-smoked salmon fillet (see below or bought)

smallish bunch of chervil

juice of 1 very juicy lemon

TO HOT-SMOKE SALMON

The best way to hot-smoke in a domestic environment is using a wok or a deep frying pan with a tight-fitting lid. If you have an electric hob, you'll need to use a flat-bottomed wok or a pan.

Lay about 600g salmon fillet, pin bones removed, in a shallow dish. Sprinkle 2 tablespoons each Demerara sugar and large-flake sea salt, and 1 teaspoon sesame oil over the flesh, and rub it in. Leave at room temperature for 30 minutes.

Line the wok tightly with 2 layers of foil at 90° to each other, each overhanging by 30cm. Sprinkle in a cup of uncooked rice (any type), a large handful of tea leaves or

untreated wood chips as fine as tea leaves, and another tablespoon of Demerara. Press firmly into the bottom. Sit a round rack inside the wok that will rest against it about 4–5cm from the base.

Wipe excess salt and sugar from the fish. Turn the extractor on full, open windows and close doors. Place the wok on a high heat with the lid off. When smoke starts to rise, lay the fish on the rack, skin side down. Put the lid on, fold the foil 'flaps' tightly over the lid, then sit a damp tea towel (you're happy to discard) on top to cover the lid completely (to catch stray smoke). Ensure this doesn't overhang as it could catch fire.

After 3 minutes, turn the heat down to medium and smoke for 7–12 minutes, depending on thickness. To test, turn heat off, peel back towel and foil, and carefully remove the lid – lots of smoke will escape so stand back. Using a small knife, prise the thickest part of the fish apart. The flesh should be a little opaque, but in a pink way. If looking completely raw, replace everything and smoke more; if opaque, remove the fish on the rack and cool on a plate.

Pour a cup of cold water into the rice to cool it down and, when cold, roll the foil into a ball and discard. You may well then decide it's easier to buy hot-smoked salmon!

WARM SALAD OF GREENSHELL MUSSELS, HIJIKI, POTATOES, WATERCRESS AND BROAD BEANS
WITH SAFFRON CUMIN DRESSING

Greenshell, or green-lipped, mussels come from New Zealand and they are larger and more meaty than the smaller European black mussels. If you can't find them fresh, frozen ones in the half-shell work very well – although, as they are already cooked, they'll just need brief reheating. Failing that, use the European mussels. Use any small potato you like, although personal favourites for this salad are Anya, Pink Fir and Baby Pearl.

600g small potatoes

salt and freshly ground black pepper

800g broad beans in the pod, podded (to give you at least 300g podded beans)

1.5kg greenshell (green-lipped) mussels in the full shell (or 1kg frozen in the half-shell, defrosted)

2 tablespoons extra-virgin olive oil

2 medium red onions, thinly sliced

2 garlic cloves, thinly sliced

2 tablespoons dried hijiki seaweed, soaked in ½ cup of water for 10 minutes

125ml dry white wine or vegetable stock

2 handfuls of watercress, roughly cut into 3cm lengths

3 spring onions, sliced into 1cm lengths

1 large juicy lemon, cut into wedges

for the saffron cumin dressing

3 tablespoons extra-virgin olive oil

1 teaspoon cumin seeds

2 good pinches of saffron, soaked in 1 teaspoon warm water

Boil the potatoes in salted water until just tender, then drain – don't refresh – and, when cool enough to handle, cut in half lengthways. Cook the broad beans in boiling salted water for about 4–6 minutes until just tender, then drain and refresh in cold water. Drain again and squeeze the green beans out of their grey skins.

While the vegetables are cooking, if your mussels are in the whole shell, rinse them thoroughly in plenty of running water, and use a blunt knife to remove any beards and barnacles that are clinging to them. Discard any that have broken shells and that stay open when tapped.

Put a large pot (which has a tight-fitting lid) over a high heat and, when it's smoking, add the olive oil, then add the onions and garlic, and sauté to colour the onions lightly. Add the drained hijiki and mussels, and give them a good stir in the pot. Add the wine and put on the lid. Cook for 3 minutes, shaking the pot twice. Take the lid off and remove any mussels that have opened and transfer to a bowl, then continue to cook until the rest open – removing them as they do. Any that haven't opened after 5 minutes should be discarded.

When the mussels are cool enough to handle, remove three-quarters of them from their shells and add the shelled mussels back to the ones in their shells. Cover the bowl with a tea towel or cling film to keep them warm for a few minutes while you assemble the dish.

Make the saffron cumin dressing, place the olive oil in a small pan over moderate heat, add the cumin seeds and cook until they turn golden, then take off the heat and add the saffron and its soaking liquid with 2 tablespoons of the mussel cooking liquor.

To serve, put everything except the saffron dressing and the lemon in a large bowl, and toss it all together, then divide between 4 bowls. Drizzle on the saffron dressing and serve with lemon wedges.

Seafood salad brings back memories of my apprenticeship in Melbourne, when it was almost the height of sophistication to serve a variety of seafood doused with a marie rose sauce – often just a tomato mayonnaise. This salad is much lighter, with no mayonnaise in sight (although I have to admit to a huge liking for the stuff) and a more modern approach to plating and ingredient selection.

Samphire is a coastal plant that tastes of crunchy brine – there are two types, with rock samphire being preferable to the not closely related marsh samphire. If you can't find it, then use fine green beans.

Your seafood has to be very fresh – avoid frozen at all costs, but also be prepared to substitute. Rather than using an old frozen langoustine, it'd be better to use fresh crab meat or lobster. Keep an eye on cooking times, as your seafood may not be as large as mine – in which case, cook it less.

SCALLOP, PRAWN AND LANGOUSTINE SALAD WITH SAMPHIRE, GRILLED AUBERGINES, SWEET POTATO, WATERCRESS AND BASIL DRESSING

Place the sweet potatoes in a large pot of cold water, salt generously and bring to the boil. Cook rapidly until you can insert a sharp knife almost into the centre. You want them three-quarters cooked. Drain and run in cold water for a minute to cool the potatoes a little. Drain and slice into 6mm rounds.

Cut the aubergines into rounds the same thickness, then brush the oil over the potatoes and aubergine slices, and lightly season. Heat a grill, skillet, barbecue or griddle pan and cook the sweet potato and aubergine slices until golden on both sides, at which point they should be cooked through. Put to one side.

Meanwhile, place the samphire in a large pot and cover with cold water. Bring to the boil and drain. Repeat, then run cold water into the pot for 2 minutes, making sure the samphire doesn't escape down the sink, then drain. Pick over to remove any woody bits and, if it's stringy, you'll have to remove the fleshy green plant from its stem. This is easy to do – just hold the fleshy body firmly between your fingers and pull it away from the stem. Put to one side.

Prepare the basil dressing, set a pot up that will hold a steamer and, when the water is boiling, add the herb to the water and boil for 5 seconds. Scoop the leaves out with a slotted spoon and put into a bowl of iced water to cool, then drain and pat dry between kitchen paper. Place the herbs in a blender with the oil and blitz to a fine purée for 10 seconds. Decant into a glass or jar.

Place the lemon peel in the boiling water and sit the steamer on top. You may need to cook in batches, but do keep in mind that overcooked seafood becomes quite chewy. Place the langoustines in the steamer, cover and cook over a rapid boil for 8 minutes (less for smaller ones). Remove from the steamer, add the prawns and cook for 1 minute, then add the scallops and cook a further 3. It is better to slightly undercook than overcook, so test a scallop by cutting it almost in half – the centre should be slightly opaque but definitely not white.

To serve, using scissors, cut down both sides of the underside of the langoustines' tails – for lobster (see page 140), removing the soft ribbed shell as you do so. Arrange the potato and aubergine slices on 4 plates. Place everything else except the dressing and lemon wedges in a large bowl and gently toss, then divide between the plates and drizzle with the basil dressing. Serve with a lemon wedge, lobster crackers and finger bowls.

2 unpeeled medium sweet potatoes, each around 250g

salt

2 medium aubergines

2 tablespoons extra-virgin olive oil

200g samphire

1 large juicy lemon, peeled and cut into 4 wedges, peel reserved

8 large langoustines

8 large prawns, heads and shells removed, apart from the tail

8 large shelled scallops, ideally walnut size, trimmed of muscle but any coral kept intact

2 handfuls of watercress

for the basil dressing
large handful of basil leaves
large handful of parsley leaves
120ml extra-virgin olive oil

Now this is an almost classic combination for anyone who's ever eaten in a Scandinavian restaurant, although the addition of tapenade leans more towards the Mediterranean.

You can save time in making this by buying pre-cooked beetroot, but if you have the time to roast them yourself it's well worth doing. Often pre-cooked beets will taste a little too acidic. Besides, if you can get hold of a variety of beets, such as golden, striped or orange, then it makes the salad all that more special. Likewise, you can buy very good tapenade, but making a batch is that much more rewarding.

Pickled herrings can be found in most good delis, either in tubs from the counter or in jars, and quality can vary greatly, so look around for the best. This salad can be served either warm or cold – let the weather on the day decide for you.

Preheat the oven to 180°C, gas 4. Wrap the beetroots tightly in foil and place in a roasting dish. Bake for 60–90 minutes (ones the size of an egg should take about 60 minutes), until you can push a thin sharp knife through the foil and into the centre of the beets. Leave to cool until you can handle them, then remove the foil and peel off the skins. You can either rub the skin off with your fingers (wear gloves or you'll have coloured hands) or use a small paring knife. Cut the beets into thin wedges or slices, place in a bowl and toss in the vinegar.

Boil or steam the potatoes then drain. When cool enough to handle, cut them into slices about 5mm thick and toss with 1 tablespoon of the olive oil.

To make the tapenade, you can use either a knife or a small food processor to roughly chop the olives, anchovies, garlic and capers (if you use baby capers there's actually no need to chop them), then mix with the lemon zest and juice, and the remaining olive oil.

To serve, toast the bread until quite crisp on both sides and divide between 4 plates. Spread the tapenade over the slices of toast, then layer the beets, potatoes and herring on top as you see fit. Add a few sprouts and serve a lemon wedge to the side.

PICKLED HERRING, BEETROOT AND POTATO SALAD ON TOASTED RYE BREAD WITH TAPENADE

700g smallish beetroots (although large ones are fine – they'll just take longer to cook), skins washed but not damaged

1 tablespoon cider vinegar or red wine vinegar

600g small waxy potatoes

3 tablespoons extra-virgin olive oil

8 large slices of rye bread or pumpernickel

8–12 pickled herring fillets, cut into small chunks

a few sprouts (see page 16)

more lemon wedges, to serve

for the tapenade

2 handfuls of stoned olives

1 salted anchovy fillet or 2 anchovy fillets in oil, drained

½ garlic clove

1 tablespoon capers, drained

2 teaspoons grated zest plus 2 tablespoons juice from 1 juicy lemon

TUNA, QUINOA, WILD ROCKET, OLIVE AND BLACKENED TOMATO SALAD
WITH CHOPPED EGG AND PARSLEY DRESSING

Before I even begin to give you this recipe I have to deliver a little rant. Please make sure the tuna you use here is from a reliable and reputable source. Tuna is, as environmentalists have said, the rhinoceros of the fish world. By that, they mean the fish is becoming hunted beyond its own ability to reproduce and survive. So, if you can't tell where the tuna you're about to buy comes from, then please make this using another species of fish, such as salmon, sea trout, mackerel or grey mullet. Also make sure it's not been caught in a drag-net, as drag-nets catch not just the tuna they're supposedly intended for, but also dolphins, sea turtles and all manner of other sea creatures. Ask your fishmonger – they should know.

That little plea over... this salad takes as its spiritual grandmother salade niçoise, using those lovely small black niçoise olives. Quinoa is an ancient Inca grain, full of all the world's goodness. Almost forgotten until recently, it has begun to appear again in health food shops and on restaurant menus.

6 tomatoes

4–5 tablespoons extra-virgin olive oil

small handful of basil leaves, torn

¾ cup quinoa grains

4 tuna steaks, each about 180g, skin and bones removed

salt and freshly ground black pepper

2 large handfuls of assorted olives

2 large handfuls of wild rocket leaves

for the chopped egg and parsley dressing

4 eggs

small handful of parsley leaves, roughly chopped

2 tablespoon capers

2 tablespoons extra-virgin olive oil

4 tablespoons lemon juice

Cut the tomatoes across into slices about 1cm thick and brush each with a little of the oil. Heat a heavy pan and, when it's smoking, add the tomatoes in a single layer and cook over a high heat to blacken a little, around 1½–2 minutes. Using a heatproof spatula, remove the slices to a plate and continue to cook the remaining slices. If any bits stick to the pan, scrape them off and wipe the pan. Once all the tomatoes are cooked, scatter the basil over them and drizzle with a teaspoon of the oil.

Bring 4 cups of water to the boil in a pan. Place the quinoa in a very fine sieve and give it a rinse under warm running water for 30 seconds. Add the quinoa to the boiling water and cook at a rapid boil for 12–15 minutes. It will be cooked when it begins to unwrap – rather like a spiral unfolding. Taste a few of the grains after 10 minutes and, once cooked, drain through a fine sieve, then spread out on a plate to cool down. The quinoa will remain slightly crunchy and nutty, and it's this texture that makes it so fabulous to use.

Brush the tuna with 2 tablespoons of the olive oil, lightly season it and leave it out at room temperature for 10 minutes, covered with cling film.

Make the chopped egg and parsley dressing, place the eggs in a pan of boiling water and boil for 5 minutes, then drain and place in a bowl of iced water to cool them completely. Shell the eggs, then roughly chop or grate them and place in a bowl with the parsley, capers- and the olive oil.

Heat the pan or grill again and, when hot, place the tuna in, or under, it and cook briefly. Tuna is best served rare to medium-rare – any more and it can become dry. However, if you like your fish overcooked and awful then, by all means, cook it so. Just don't say I told you to. For a steak that's 1½ cm thick, to cook it medium-rare in a hot pan will take about 2 minutes on the first side, then flipped over and cooked for a further minute.

To serve, place the olives, rocket and quinoa in a large bowl, lightly season, add the remaining olive oil and gently mix. Lay the tomato slices on 4 plates and divide the rocket salad on top of that, then top with a piece of grilled tuna. Mix the lemon juice into the egg dressing and spoon this over as you serve it.

Ceviche – fish 'cooked' in a marinade of citrus juice – can be made from almost any fish, but fish fillets that are too thin can fall apart and look a little sad. Ideally, choose a sustainable fish that has some grunt to it, something with generous flakes and flavour, such as haddock or snapper.

Tomatillos, also known as Mexican tomatoes, are actually close relatives of the cape gooseberry or physalis fruit. Round and green, sometimes ripening to yellow, they have a delicious flavour of lemons and apples. Increasingly widely available here, like their fruity relative they come shrouded in a protective husk that needs to be removed.

This is the perfect summer meal to follow a bowl of chilled gazpacho.

CEVICHE OF COD
WITH CUCUMBER, LIME, TOMATILLO, BASIL AND MINT

600g cod fillet, skin and any small bones removed

1 teaspoon of finely grated zest and 100 ml juice from 3–4 juicy limes

sea salt

1 cucumber, about 25cm long

3 large tomatillos, husks and stems removed

½ red or green chilli (the heat level is up to you), finely chopped

1 grapefruit, peeled and segmented (see page 150)

handful of basil

small handful of small Thai basil leaves

4 spring onions, thinly sliced and rinsed in cold water

2 tablespoons extra-virgin olive oil

Cut the cod fillet into strips about 2cm thick, then cut these into cubes and place in a non-reactive bowl. Add half the lime zest, half the juice and ¼ teaspoon of salt, and mix well. Cover and place in the fridge for 2 hours.

Meanwhile, peel the cucumber and slice lengthways, then scoop out the seeds with a teaspoon and discard. Cut the cucumber into rough 2cm cubes and mix in a bowl with ½ teaspoon of salt. Toss well, cover and place in the fridge.

About 20 minutes before serving, take the fish and cucumber from the fridge. Carefully tip the fish into a colander and discard the juices that run from it. Drain the liquid from the cucumber, rinse it briefly under cold water and then tip on top of the fish and leave them both to drain for 5 minutes.

Cut the tomatillos into slices about ½cm thick, then toss with a teaspoon of the lime juice, a few pinches of salt and the chilli.

Put the fish mixture into a clean bowl, add the remaining lime zest and juice, together with the chillies and tomatillos, and mix together. Cover again and put in the fridge for 10 minutes.

Just before serving, add the grapefruit, basil, Thai basil, spring onions and olive oil, and mix gently. Taste and adjust the seasoning as necessary, then divide between 4 bowls.

If you can't find tomatillos, don't despair – chunks of mango added at the last minute will add a tropical touch to the ceviche. Freshly grated green papaya or mango will add a Thai edge, and diced Nashi pears or jícama (yam bean) also make a great textural and tasty addition. Even slightly underripe tomatoes, thinly sliced, will add a crunchy freshness.

CRAB CLAW, CUCUMBER, LIME, WATERCRESS, CORIANDER, NEW POTATO AND WASABI MAYONNAISE SALAD

Crab claws are a real hands-on eating experience. You'll have to pick them up and suck out the flesh, use your teeth to clamp on to the meat inside and use your fingers and a solid toothpick, or special crab pick, to get at the meat in the corners. However, it's well worth it: it's fun and it's sociable. But… if you don't want to serve this for a formal diner, then buy crab meat already taken from the shell.

Wasabi is one of those flavours that either you get or you don't. I get it, and I like to get it hot and fiery. But you can always make the mayonnaise moderately hot and serve extra wasabi on the side so as not to offend your more delicate guests.

Finely grate the zest of 1 of the limes and then juice both to give you 4 tablespoons of juice. Shred the cucumber into fine julienne strips with a knife or mandolin grater, avoiding the seeds, or slice it very thinly into discs. Mix with half the lime juice and the zest, and all of the mirin, and place in the fridge for an hour to pickle lightly.

Mix the wasabi powder with the remaining lime juice, then mix into the mayonnaise. Season well. Mix the potato halves with half the mayonnaise, then toss with the chives, red onion and coriander.

To serve, divide the potato salad between 4 plates and scatter the watercress on top. Pile the cucumber on that, then lastly poke 3 crab claws into each plate. Spoon the remaining mayonnaise into a bowl and allow your friends to serve themselves.

2 juicy limes

1 large cucumber

2 tablespoons mirin

1 teaspoon wasabi powder (more or less to taste)

125ml mayonnaise

salt and freshly ground black pepper

500g baby new potatoes, cooked and refreshed, then halved

3 tablespoons thinly sliced chives

1 medium red onion, very thinly sliced and rinsed in cold water for a minute

handful of coriander leaves

2 large handfuls of watercress

12 crab claws, cooked and shells cracked (ask your fishmonger to prepare these)

Poultry Salads
using chicken, turkey, duck, quail and other birds

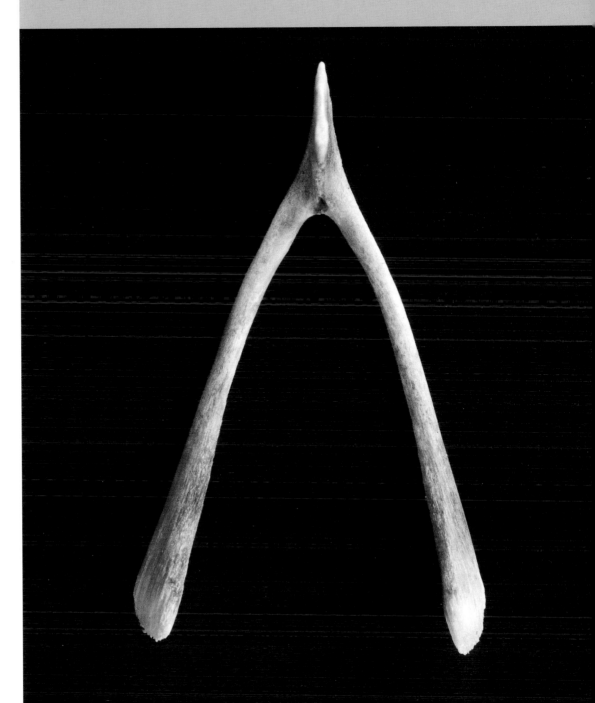

LEFTOVER ROAST CHICKEN, PASTA, OAK LEAF, BEAN AND CHÈVRE SALAD WITH TOMATO GINGER DRESSING

This is one of those 'what is there to eat' meals that we all experience at some time or another, when you open the fridge door and hope something's left from last night's dinner. You'd need at least half a chicken to feed 4 people, so if you have a little less you'll need to bulk it out with extra pasta, beans, peas, tomatoes etc., or just serve the salad with lots of bread spread generously with butter mixed with finely chopped garlic that has been grilled or baked until golden.

As for the type of pasta to use, there are limitless possibilities these days, but I'd recommend a short rather than a spaghetti-type pasta – something like fusilli, penne or farfalle. If it's a cold day outside, you can serve this salad warm simply by using freshly cooked pasta straight from the pot and chicken that you've gently warmed in a pan or in the oven.

flesh from approximately ½ cooked chicken

1 medium oak leaf lettuce, leaves separated

2 heads of red chicory (also called red endive), leaves separated

200g pasta (see above), cooked in salted boiling water until just tender but still firm to the bite, drained and refreshed in cold water

200g green beans, blanched in boiling water for 2 minutes and refreshed in cold water

200g chèvre (goats' cheese, but you can use another suitable crumbly cheese, such as feta or Wensleydale, if you prefer)

for the tomato ginger dressing

3 large ripe tomatoes

piece of peeled ginger about 1x2cm, or 1 ball of stem ginger

2 tablespoons lemon juice

125ml olive oil

salt and freshly ground black pepper

2 tablespoons extra-virgin olive oil

First make the dressing, place the tomatoes, ginger, lemon juice and olive oil in a blender and whiz on high speed for 30 seconds. The finished dressing should be lump-free. Taste and adjust the seasoning, then add the extra-virgin olive oil and whiz for another 5 seconds.

Cut the chicken flesh across the grain into nut-sized chunks and place in a bowl. Cut the larger oak leaves into 5cm pieces and add to the bowl; keep the smaller inside ones whole and set side to finish the salad. Add the drained cooked pasta and the beans. Either cut the chèvre into small chunks with a knife or break it apart with your fingers and add the pieces to the bowl.

To serve, mix all the salad ingredients together and divide between 4 bowls. Scatter them with the reserved inside leaves and drizzle with the dressing.

This salad needn't just be based on leftovers – or chicken. If you don't happen to have any roast chicken to use up, the dressing goes with a myriad other flavours. Try it with a freshly roasted chicken breast or boned thigh, thinly sliced leftover roast lamb, sliced barbecued or grilled pork chops, grilled best-quality sausages cut into chunks, or go vegetarian by using chunks of roast pumpkin, squash or sweet potato.

PANKO-CRUMBED TURKEY, HONEY-GLAZED PARSNIP AND WATERCRESS SALAD, CRANBERRY POMEGRANATE COMPOTE AND A DEEP-FRIED EGG

This warm meal is best served around Christmas time. It's actually great served as an alternative Christmas lunch if you really can't be bothered with cooking a whole bird and you want a lighter meal. We've been serving deep-fried eggs at The Providores for almost four years now and they are one of our most surprising dishes. Our customers are divided into two camps – those that get it, and those that don't. I love them. Panko are breadcrumbs from Japan – they're coarser and longer than regular breadcrumbs and they give added texture to the turkey. If you can't find panko (also look for honey panko), the next best thing is to grate a few slices of two-day-old unflavoured sourdough, which should also give you nice coarse threads.

5 eggs

flour for coating

4 turkey steaks, each about 220g

2 handfuls of panko crumbs (see above)

vegetable oil for cooking

500g watercress, large stems removed

for the honey-glazed parsnips

salt and freshly ground black pepper

500g smallish parsnips, peeled and cut lengthways into wedges

2 tablespoons runny honey

70g butter

15 sage leaves, shredded

125ml hot water

for the cranberry and pomegranate compote

50g unrefined caster sugar

5 tablespoons pomegranate molasses

¼ teaspoon cayenne pepper or paprika

1 tablespoon mustard seeds

200g cranberries (both fresh and frozen will work)

First make the honey-glazed parsnips, preheat the oven to 190°C, gas 5. Line a baking dish (just large enough to hold the parsnips) with baking parchment, lay the parsnips in it and lightly season. Add the honey, butter, sage and hot water. Seal tightly with foil or a lid and bake until you can insert a small sharp knife through the thickest part of the parsnip, about 40 minutes. Once tender, remove the foil and bake until they take on a golden hue.

Meanwhile, make the cranberry-pomegranate compote, bring the sugar, molasses, cayenne pepper and mustard seeds to the boil in a small pan, then add the cranberries and a little salt, gently stirring. You want half the cranberries to burst, but not all or you'll have a pan of mush! Take off the heat.

Bring a pan of water to the boil and carefully add 4 of the eggs with a slotted spoon. Boil for 4 minutes only – adjust this time depending on their size. Remove the eggs from the pan and place in a bowl, then let cold water run over them for 5 minutes to cool them completely. Shell and keep in the fridge.

Season the flour and use to coat the steaks one at a time. Whisk the remaining egg and dip the steaks into this one at a time. Lay the panko on a plate and coat the turkey evenly on both sides in that, pressing the crumbs in so they adhere.

Heat 2 tablespoons of oil in a frying pan to medium and cook the turkey until golden on both sides. If your pan is large you may be able to cook them all at once; if not, cook them in two batches. In total, a 1cm thick steak should take around 8 minutes. To test if it's cooked, cut into the thickest part and carefully pull apart. When it's white in colour, it's ready. Bear in mind that turkey gets quite dry if overcooked, so keep an eye on it. Keep warm.

Heat a deep-fryer or a pan with 5cm of oil to 180°C. Pat the eggs dry and carefully lower them into the oil with a slotted spoon. Cook until golden, around 4-5 minutes – you want them to have a runny centre, so again keep an eye on them. Remove from the oil and place on kitchen paper to drain.

To serve, place the turkey on warm plates. Mix the watercress with the parsnips and any roasting pan juices, and divide between 4 plates. Dollop on the compote and finally sit a halved egg in the centre of the plate.

The quickest way to make this salad is to buy a roast duck from your nearest Chinatown. Otherwise, roast a duck yourself (or roast one breast per person), which is actually just as easy as roasting a chicken.

Season the cavity of the duck and sit it on top of a few carrots and sliced onions in a roasting tray, breast down. Pour on half a cup of boiling water and season well. Roast at 180°C, gas 4, for 30 minutes, then turn over and roast, breast up, until cooked – about another 50 minutes for a 1.5kg bird. It is cooked when you insert a sharp knife into the thigh and the juices run clear. For the last 5 minutes, place it under the grill in the oven, if you can, to crisp up the skin. Allow to rest for at least 15 minutes before cutting.

In summer I serve this at room temperature, but in winter I serve the duck straight from the oven and the corn hot from the pan. Romanesco, which is a winter broccoli, can then be replaced with regular broccoli or cauliflower.

Preheat the oven to 170°C, gas 3½. Mix the walnuts, spice and maple syrup in a small bowl and lay on a baking tray lined with non-stick parchment. Bake in the centre of the oven until golden and baked through, around 12–18 minutes, tossing them occasionally, then remove and leave to cool.

Meanwhile, if you're using a whole duck you'll need to get the meat off the carcass. It's a matter of using a small sharp knife and your fingers to pull and cut all the flesh from the bones. Take off the legs first and remove their bones by cutting lengthways down the thigh and drumstick, then pulling them out. Take the two breasts off the carcass one at a time. Cut the meat into slices or small chunks and put to one side.

Toss the sweetcorn with the oil and fry them in a hot pan to colour them slightly all over, shaking the pan to allow them to cook evenly. Remove from the pan and put in a bowl.

Segment the oranges (see page 150), reserving the juice that runs off, and place the segments in a bowl with the corn and romanesco. Slice the fennel thinly on a mandolin grater (or use a sharp knife) and add this to the corn. Remove the leaves from the radicchio and add these to the salad bowl.

Make the soy tahini dressing, whisk the reserved orange juice with the soy sauce, tahini and olive oil so that the mixture emulsifies, or shake it all together in a jar, and adjust the seasoning.

To serve, lay the duck on top of the salad, scatter with the sesame seeds and pass the bowl around with a jug of the dressing.

DUCK SALAD WITH ORANGES, MAPLE WALNUTS, BABY CORN, ROMANESCO, RADICCHIO AND FENNEL, SOY TAHINI DRESSING

2 large handfuls of walnuts

2 pinches of ground cinnamon or nutmeg

2 tablespoons maple syrup

1 whole duck, cooked as above, or 4 duck breasts, cooked to medium-rare

20 baby sweetcorn

1 teaspoon olive oil

3 large juicy oranges

1 head of romanesco, separated, blanched and refreshed in iced water

1 head of fennel

1 medium head of radicchio

2 teaspoons toasted sesame seeds

for the soy tahini dressing

3 tablespoons soy sauce

3 tablespoons tahini

5 teaspoons olive oil

POACHED CHICKEN, HAZELNUT, WATERCRESS AND PEA SALAD WITH LEMON GRASS DRESSING

A simple salad like this relies on the best and very freshest ingredients. Buy the most expensive, high-quality chicken that you can afford – you'll be glad you did once you've tasted the finished product. If you can't get hold of lemon grass, then use the equivalent amount of finely grated lemon zest in the dressing and use lemon peel in the poaching liquor.

Cut the base 2cm up from the bottom of each lemon grass stalk, then cut the end off, leaving you with two 5cm pieces. Peel the outer tough 2 or 3 layers off these and put the base, ends and outer layers into a large deep pot (one that'll just hold the chicken comfortably). Remove 1 heaped teaspoon of the thyme leaves from the stems and put to one side, then add the thyme, oregano, bay leaves, garlic, celery, carrot, wine and a little salt to the pot and pour in 2.5 litres of water. Bring to the boil, then simmer and cook for 10 minutes.

Remove the legs and thighs from the chicken and add to the stock. Bring to the boil, then simmer for 10 minutes. Add the carcass and bring back to the boil, then again turn down to a rapid simmer and cook for 18 minutes (for a 1.5kg bird – it'll be a little longer for a larger bird). To check to see if it's ready, as the bird will finish cooking in the liquor, remove one of the legs from the stock and cut into the thickest part – it should be almost cooked through; if it's still a little raw-looking, then keep simmering for another 5 minutes before turning the heat off. If it's looking almost cooked, then turn the heat off and leave to cool completely in the stock with a lid on the pot.

While the chicken is cooking, preheat the oven to 170°C, gas3½. Place the hazelnuts on a baking tray and cook until golden – around 10–15 minutes, shaking them as they cook to colour them evenly. Remove from the oven, turn it off and leave to cool. Finely chop one-third of the hazelnuts with a knife or grind in a small food processor and keep to one side.

Slice the tender inner parts of the lemon grass as thinly as you can and put in a jar with the lemon juice, olive oil and a little seasoning. Put the lid on and give it a good shake.

Once the chicken has cooled in the stock, remove it and drain the stock through a fine sieve (see note right). Using your fingers or a knife, remove the meat from the legs and carcass of the chicken, then break or slice into chunks.

To serve, add the ground hazelnuts to the dressing and shake well again. Mix the peas with the watercress and the remaining hazelnuts and divide among 4 plates, then sit the chicken pieces on top. Shake the dressing one last time and pour it over the chicken, making sure all plates get an even serving of the lemon grass.

2 lemon grass stalks

large handful of fresh thyme

small handful of fresh oregano

2 bay leaves

4 garlic cloves, peeled and halved

2 celery stalks, each cut into 4

1 large carrot, quartered

1 glass of white wine

1 large chicken, about 1.5–1.8kg)

large handful of skinned hazelnuts

1 tablespoon lemon juice

4 tablespoons olive oil

3 handfuls of peas, blanched and refreshed in cold water

2 bunches of watercress, thick stems removed

Note Putting the stock back on to boil and letting it reduce by three-quarters will give you a lovely broth to be used for a soup or some other recipe. The quickest way to do this is in a wide pot, as the more surface area you have the quicker it will evaporate. Once it has reduced, let it cool completely before putting in the fridge or freezer.

WARM SALAD OF POUSSIN POACHED IN SOY, STAR ANISE AND BLACK VINEGAR WITH BABY CARROTS, TAT SOI AND SHIITAKE

2 poussins, each about 450g

300ml soy sauce

100g dark or pale palm sugar
(or a high-molasses cane sugar)

8 star anise

1 tablespoon Sichuan peppercorns

125ml black vinegar

8 garlic cloves, crushed

3 fingers of fresh ginger, skin
scrubbed

4 tablespoons lemon juice

20 baby carrots (you can peel them
or just wash them well)

20 shiitake mushrooms

1 tablespoon vegetable oil

2 tablespoons sesame oil

2 large handfuls tat soi (or use bok
choy or pak choy)

3 spring onions, thinly sliced at
an angle

3 tablespoons crispy shallots (see
page 12)

handful of picked coriander

The cooking method here can be used for any poultry (see also the poached chicken recipe on the previous page) – just keep in mind that the larger the bird the longer you'll need to cook it. The stock in which it is cooked is called a 'master stock'. That's because, in Chinese restaurants especially (and most restaurants where I have poached poultry), the stock is used again and again, and each time the flavour intensifies and becomes better and better.

A poussin is a small chicken, usually weighing 400–500g. It's important you cook the poussin as directed below – any less and it may be undercooked; any more and it could become a little dry. You can serve this salad warm or cold – so long as you feel comfortable portioning a warm bird; just remember it may be a little slippery, so handle it with care.

Take any trussing string off the birds and rinse them under cool running water for a minute, then drain and wipe the cavity dry with kitchen paper.

Place 2 litres of water, the soy sauce, sugar, star anise, Sichuan peppercorns, all but 2 tablespoons of the vinegar, and the garlic into a pot just large enough to hold the birds comfortably. Slice 2 fingers of the ginger and add to the pot. Bring to the boil, then simmer for 15 minutes. Place in the poussins, breast side down, and bring back to the boil. Reduce to a bubbling simmer and poach for 14 minutes; turn the birds over and poach for a further 5 minutes. Cover the pot, take off the heat and leave to cool.

Peel the remaining ginger and thinly slice it (a mandolin grater is good for this), then cut the slices into fine julienne strips and mix with the lemon juice. Put to one side.

Once the poussins have cooled, remove them from the stock, strain it and put it back on to boil. Add the carrots and boil them until half cooked (slightly crunchy carrots are good in this dish), then remove them with a slotted spoon and leave to cool. Let the stock cool completely before storing in the fridge (so long as you use it once every week), or freeze it. Every time you reuse it, check the seasoning and add either more soy sauce or water as taste dictates.

Remove the stems from the mushrooms, score an 'X' in the cap and sauté in the vegetable and sesame oils until softened. Add the reserved black vinegar at the end and leave to cool.

Now you need to portion your poussins. You can either just simply cut them through the backbone using a pair of kitchen shears and serve 1 half per person, or you can remove the legs, cutting each in half through the knee joint, and then remove the breast from the carcass and serve a breast and 2 leg halves per person.

To serve, mix the tat soi with half the lemon-marinated ginger and all of the carrots, the shiitake and the spring onions. Divide this salad between the plates, then lay the pieces of poussin on top. Scatter on the remaining ginger and lemon juice, the crispy shallots and the coriander, and pour a few tablespoons of the master stock over as you serve it.

STEAMED CHICKEN, FLAGEOLET BEAN, ROAST PLUM TOMATO AND FENNEL SALAD
WITH TRUFFLED LEMON DRESSING

This salad is perfect for lunch on a sunny day. The chicken can be either served straight from the steamer or left to cool. The bean and fennel salad also makes a great accompaniment to roast or poached chicken. You can make the salad using freshly cooked beans, such as broad beans, borlotti or cannellini, or save time by using canned ones. Also try making this as a meat-free starter, with a little hard cheese shaved on top, or try it with grilled squid or prawns replacing the chicken.

8–12 plum tomatoes

1½ tablespoons extra-virgin olive oil

salt and freshly ground black pepper

4 boneless chicken breasts

2 heads of fennel

400g can of cooked flageolet beans, drained and rinsed

1 small red onion, thinly sliced

handful of beansprouts, rinsed

handful of flat-leaf parsley

2 tablespoons lemon juice

small handful of sprouts (see page 16) or cress (I used what is called onion cress)

for the truffled lemon dressing

2 tablespoons soy sauce

1½ tablespoons extra-virgin olive oil

1 tablespoon truffle oil

2 tablespoons lemon juice

Preheat the oven to 180°C, gas 4, and line a baking tray with baking parchment. Cut the tomatoes in half lengthways and place on the tray, cut side up. Drizzle with the olive oil, season lightly and bake until they colour and shrink a little, 90 minutes. (If after about an hour they start to colour too much, cover with foil.)

About 30 minutes before they're going to be ready, get a steamer steaming and place the lightly seasoned chicken breasts in it with the heat up full. Cook until the thickest part of the breast is just cooked (around 12–18 minutes depending on size – use a sharp knife to cut into it and check if it's ready). Take from the steamer and leave to cool to room temperature, covered in cling film or foil.

Thinly shave the fennel and place in iced water to crisp up.

Make the truffled lemon dressing: mix together the soy sauce, olive oil, truffle oil and lemon juice. Taste and adjust the seasoning, if necessary.

Mix the beans with the onion, beansprouts, parsley and lemon juice and lightly season.

To serve, divide the bean salad between 4 plates and sit the tomato halves on top. Slice each chicken breast into 4 pieces and sit these on top of the salad. Toss the fennel with the dressing and place on the chicken, then sprinkle with the sprouts.

Quails are birds that you really need to get your fingers on to appreciate. They are obviously small, with bones that are sometimes annoying, but they are juicy and tasty when cooked properly. The rule of thumb is never to overcook them. If you can buy them boned out, then use those; if you can only find whole birds, then simply prepare them as follows.

Place them, one at a time, in the palm of your hand, breast side down. You'll have the quail's backbone facing up to you, running from the neck cavity to the abdomen cavity. Using a pair of scissors, cut along either side of the backbone, about a centimetre apart, and then pull the backbone out and away from the bird. Now lay the bird on a board, breast side up, and press it into the board to flatten it. This is called 'spatchcocking'.

Although this recipe calls for barbecuing the quails and aubergines, you can also do it successfully in your kitchen on a heavy skillet or grill.

BARBECUED THYME-MARINATED QUAIL ON A SALAD OF SWEETCORN, AUBERGINE, RED CHICORY, PEAR AND GREEN OLIVES

8 quails, spatchcocked as above

small handful of fresh thyme on the stem (or 1 teaspoon dried thyme)

1 garlic clove, thinly chopped or crushed

4 tablespoons extra-virgin olive oil

2 tablespoons soy sauce

salt and freshly ground black pepper

2 corn cobs, outer husks removed

2 medium aubergines

1 teaspoon sesame oil

2 heads of red chicory (also called red endive)

2 pears

handful of green olives

handful of cress or sprouts (see page 16)

2 juicy lemons, halved

Put the quails into a large bowl and add the thyme, garlic, 1 tablespoon of the olive oil, all of the soy sauce and a little freshly ground pepper, then rub this all over the birds. Leave to marinate for 1 hour at room temperature (if the room is hot, then pop them in the fridge).

Bring a large pot of salted water to the boil and cook the corn cobs for 4–5 minutes (4 if they're really fresh), then drain.

Cut the aubergines into slices about 1cm thick and mix the sesame oil into the remaining oil. Brush 2 tablespoons of this oil over both sides of the aubergine slices and barbecue them on both sides until done. The aubergines are cooked when they are golden brown and you can easily push your finger into them. Remove and place on a plate.

Once the quails are ready to cook, take them from the marinade and cook on the barbecue, skin side up, over a moderate heat – too fierce and they may blacken on the outside without cooking on the inside. Turn over after 4 minutes; they should be nicely charred but definitely not burnt. Cook for around 2 minutes on the other side. The degree of heat you are cooking over and the fact that the quails may or may not be boned, will affect the cooking time. But, as with all birds on the bone, just poke a sharp knife into the thickest part, near the thigh bone, to see if it's cooked through. The meat will look brown/red and have no signs of rawness. If the breasts are a little pink, all the better, as they will be juicy and tender. Once they're cooked, remove them from the barbecue and place on a plate.

Cut the corn into rounds about 1cm thick. Cut the bases from the chicory heads and separate all the leaves. Remove the cores from the pears and peel if you want to, then cut each into 8 wedges.

To serve, place the corn and aubergine on 4 plates. Mix the chicory, pears, olives, cress or sprouts and remaining oil in a bowl, then sit this salad on top. Cut the quails in half lengthways, then remove the legs from the breasts and sit 2 quartered birds on top of each plate of salad. Serve with a wedge of lemon.

WARM DUCK LEG SALAD WITH COCONUT, CORIANDER, RED PEPPERS, NOODLES, CHINESE CABBAGE AND HONEY-GLAZED CASHEWS

Duck legs, like chicken legs, are a more muscular part of the bird and therefore tend to have more flavour than the breast, but as the muscle makes them tougher they benefit from being cooked slowly, as in this braising method. French duck confit (cooked in its own fat over a low heat for many hours) is perhaps the most common of European way of cooking the leg, but I have had far more delicious legs in northern Thailand, where they were simmered in a wok-like pot in lots of duck fat with the addition of copious amounts of star anise, garlic and ginger. Either way, the lengthy cooking process required to get them tender is well worth it. If you don't have the time, head to your nearest deli and buy some duck confit.

Black cardamom pods have a lovely earthy taste that imparts a subtle smoky flavour; if you can't find them, don't despair, simply use regular green cardamom and perhaps a pinch of pimenton (Spanish smoked paprika). See page 149 on how to extract coconut meat from the shell.

6 large duck legs on the bone, each about 180g

1 medium-hot red chilli, quartered lengthways

4 garlic cloves, sliced

6 star anise

4 black cardamom pods

1 tablespoon coriander seeds

400ml unsweetened coconut milk

3 tablespoons Thai fish sauce

300ml hot water

200g cashew nuts

2 teaspoons runny honey

1/2 teaspoon vegetable oil

4 red peppers

100g rice noodles

3 juicy limes

salt

1/2 Chinese cabbage, shredded

3 spring onions, thinly sliced and rinsed

large handful of picked coriander leaves

1/2 fresh coconut, thinly shaved (or use a handful of wide-thread desiccated coconut) and lightly toasted

Preheat the oven to 180°C, gas 4. Heat a dry frying pan and brown the duck legs over a moderate heat on both sides, draining off the fat every few minutes. You won't need to add any oil. Once browned, place them in a casserole dish large enough to hold them in one layer.

Keep 1/2 teaspoon of the fat in the pan and add the chilli, garlic, star anise, cardamom and coriander seeds, and sauté until the garlic is golden. Add the coconut milk, fish sauce and hot water, and bring to the boil. Pour over the legs, seal tightly with a lid or foil and bake in the centre of the oven for 90 minutes.

Mix the cashew nuts with the honey and oil and spread in a single layer on a tray lined with non-stick baking parchment, then bake for 12–15 minutes. The nuts burn quite easily, so you need to keep an eye on them, lightly mixing them on the tray from time to time. Once they've turned golden (it pays to break one open to make sure it's coloured right through), take from the oven and let cool completely on the tray before storing in an airtight jar.

Grill or roast the peppers to blacken the skins, turning frequently, then place in a sealed plastic bag and leave to cool. Once cool, peel off the skin, discard the stem and seeds, and cut the flesh into strips.

Prepare the noodles by pouring barely boiling water over them in a heatproof bowl and leave to soak. Juice 2 of the limes and cut the third into quarters.

Once the duck legs are ready, remove the dish from the oven and take out the legs. Strain the coconut mixture through a fine sieve into a 1 litre jug and skim off the fat – there will be a lot. Add the lime juice, taste for seasoning and keep warm.

When the legs are cool enough to handle, remove the meat and skin from the bones and break or cut it into chunks – you'll find it comes away easily. If you don't like the idea of eating the skin then discard it, but it is very tasty.

To serve, drain the noodles and mix with the peppers, cabbage, spring onions and half the cashew nuts, then divide between 4 plates. Mix the duck meat with half the coriander, and place this on the noodles. Scatter on the remaining nuts, coriander and coconut, place a lime segment on the side and serve the coconut dressing in a jug.

STEAMED GUINEA FOWL, ASPARAGUS, PRESERVED LEMON AND TARRAGON SALAD WITH WILD ROCKET AND GRAIN MUSTARD AVOCADO DRESSING

Guinea fowl aren't frequently used, yet they're as easy to cook as a regular chicken. They have a similar flavour to free-range chicken, but have subtle differences that make it worthwhile experimenting with them. They are quite lean, so do make sure you don't overcook them. Preserved lemons – preserved in salt and lemon juice – are increasingly easy to find in good delis and Middle Eastern shops, but they can be made very easily at home.

When I steam food at home I tend to use a bamboo steamer from Asia, but you'll also be able to use a metal purpose-built one, or one of those electric plastic ones that are more common these days. One tip when steaming is that if you flavour the water with aromatics, such as herbs, tea or spices, some of the flavour will be imparted into the steamed product. I always steam birds with the skin on – if you're on some diet that won't allow you to eat the skin, then still steam the bird with the skin on and take it off once cooked – it'll help keep the bird moist and add flavour.

Lightly season the guinea fowl all over and put to one side. Set up a steamer with 5cm of water in the bottom – ideally you want to be able to steam all the breasts together in one layer, so they cook evenly.

Snap the asparagus spears by holding either end between the thumb and forefinger of each hand and gently bending them towards each other. The end with the tip is the good tender piece; the other end will be a little woody, although you can peel it with a potato peeler. Place the woody end in the steamer water.

Using a sharp knife, cut the rind from the preserved lemon – it is easiest to do this by cutting the lemon half in half again, lengthways, and then sitting it, rind side down, on a chopping board. Poke your knife in at one of the ends, then cut the fleshy bit out as you run the knife parallel to the board. Place the fleshy bit in the steamer water.

Remove the tarragon leaves from the stems and place the stems in the water. Turn the steamer on and, when it's boiling, place the asparagus in and cook for 4 minutes. Take out and put on a plate to cool.

Next, steam the breasts, place them in the steamer, skin side up, and steam. They should take between 12 and 15 minutes, depending on thickness. To see if they're cooked, remove one breast and lay it on a chopping board. Poke a thin sharp knife into the thickest part of the breast and cut through into the centre. The meat should be white – if it's a little opaque, continue steaming until it's done. Remove the breasts from the steamer and put on a plate.

While the breasts are steaming, chop the preserved lemon rind into small dice and mix with the tarragon leaves and rocket.

Make the grain mustard and avocado dressing, place one-third of the avocado flesh in a food processor or blender (or use a hand mixer), add the other ingredients and blitz to a smooth purée. Season. Using a fork or potato masher, roughly mash the remaining flesh with a little seasoning.

To serve, dollop the avocado mash on 4 plates. Slice the asparagus at an angle and add to the rocket, tarragon, lemon and olive oil. Toss together, then mound on top of the avocado. Slice the breasts at an angle into 5–6 pieces and lay on top of the salad, then spoon on the dressing and sprinkle with the sprouts.

4 guinea fowl breasts

salt and freshly ground black pepper

24 medium asparagus stalks

1/2 preserved lemon

6 tarragon stems

2 large handfuls of wild rocket

2 tablespoons extra-virgin olive oil

small handful of sprouts (see page 16)

for the grain mustard avocado dressing

2 avocados, halved, stoned and flesh scooped out

3 tablespoons lime juice

2 tablespoons grain mustard

3 tablespoons avocado oil

Meat and Game Salads based on beef, lamb, pork, sausage, bacon, offal and venison

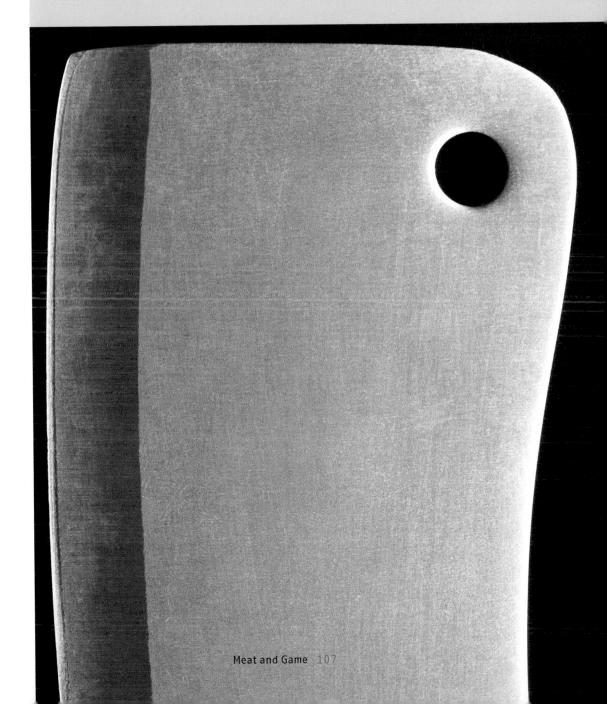

WARM SALAD OF CALVES' LIVER, MUSHROOMS, LEEK AND POTATO WITH CHILLIED WHISKY PRUNE DRESSING

This salad is another good cold-weather lunch or dinner. Calves' liver has a fabulous texture and a wonderful flavour and, when combined with the other ingredients here, especially the whisky, it becomes a warming meal. If you can't get calves' liver, then it can be made with duck livers or, at a stretch, chicken livers, although these have a much lighter flavour. If you're not a fan of whisky, or you don't have any in the house, then use brandy or dark rum instead – or just leave it out.

600g calves' liver

salt and freshly ground black pepper

300g small potatoes

300g mixed mushrooms (I used small field, shiitake and shimeji mushrooms)

50g butter

5 tablespoons olive oil

1 leek, thinly sliced

1 chilli, thinly sliced

2 garlic cloves, chopped

12 small pitted prunes, halved (I used delicious juicy Pruneaux d'Agen)

2–3 shots of whisky

handful of rocket

Slice the liver into pieces 1.5cm thick. Season it liberally and leave to rest on a plate.

Boil the potatoes until tender, then drain and slice in half (although you can keep them whole if they're small enough). If the mushrooms you have are large, then tear or slice them into evenly sized pieces.

Heat a large wide pan and add the butter and half the olive oil. Bring to a bubbling sizzle, then add the liver and cook for 4 minutes over a moderate heat. Flip over and cook for another 3 minutes – this will give you liver that's cooked to just beyond medium-rare. If you like yours cooked more, then do so. To check to see what stage it is at, cut into the centre of the liver with a sharp knife and prise the liver apart. Remove from the pan and place in a warm dish and keep covered – you might like to put it in a low oven to keep it warm.

Remove any burnt bits from the pan but don't wipe it out. Add the leek to the pan with 1 tablespoon of the oil and sauté to soften, then add the potatoes and warm them through. Tip on to a warm plate.

Add the remaining oil to the pan and then sauté the mushrooms until wilted. Add the chilli, garlic and prunes, and cook for 2 minutes, stirring well. Add the whisky and bring to the boil, then take off the heat.

To serve, divide the leek and potato mixture between 4 plates, then sit the rocket on top. Slice the liver at an angle and sit this on top, then place the warm mushroom salad on that and pour over any juices that have collected from the pan or the plate with the liver.

This salad is good to serve on a cold day. The flavours are robust and earthy, with the beef complementing the 'greens' especially well. The salad can also be made with grilled sirloin or rump steak, roast lamb (loin or leg) or venison (fillet works best). If using venison, both wild and farmed will taste great – but don't cook the wild more than quite rare as it will toughen.

Salsify is a very odd-looking vegetable, as it is a long root which usually comes covered in dirt. It has black skin, white flesh and a taste not too dissimilar to celeriac and artichokes. If you can't find any, then use roast Jerusalem artichokes or celeriac, braised globe artichokes, or just potatoes.

Fresh horseradish has a wonderful aroma and flavour, but if it's too hard to get a hold of then use a good-quality horseradish from a jar. If you do get hold of the fresh stuff, then just grate what you need, once peeled, from the root and keep the rest tightly wrapped in the fridge – it will last at least a month if looked after properly.

RARE BEEF FILLET SALAD WITH FRESH HORSERADISH, SORREL, RADICCHIO, SALSIFY AND FIELD MUSHROOMS

800g beef fillet, trimmed of all sinew and fat

salt and freshly ground black pepper

5 tablespoons extra-virgin olive oil

2 lemons

4 salsify roots, around 600g in total

8 large field mushrooms, sliced

1 small head of radicchio, thinly sliced (what is referred to as a chiffonade)

bunch of sorrel, stalks removed

2 tablespoons freshly grated horseradish (more or less to taste)

Lightly season the beef fillet and rub with a tablespoon of the olive oil. Cover and leave at room temperature while you are preparing the rest of the ingredients.

Bring a pot of lightly salted water to the boil with one of the lemons sliced into it to help prevent the salsify discolouring. Wash the dirt from the salsify under cold running water, cut both ends off and peel it. As you peel each one, cut them into pieces that will easily fit into the pot and place them in it, turning the heat down to a simmer. Once you've peeled them all, turn the heat under the pot back up to a gentle boil and cook until tender – you should be able to insert a thin sharp knife into them as you would a potato. Drain and leave to cool.

Heat a heavy frying pan, skillet or grill and cook the beef to colour on all sides. For this dish, I cooked the fillet in one piece, then sliced it as I was serving it. You may prefer to cook it in steaks and serve them whole – I leave it to you. To cook one large piece of fillet to just beyond rare, cook it on all sides, turning every minute to cook it evenly all over. Allow it to rest in a warm place for at least 15 minutes – this will help the meat be juicy.

If you used a pan to sear the meat, then use it to cook the mushrooms; otherwise heat a fresh pan, add half the remaining olive oil and sauté the mushrooms over a moderate heat to soften them – they'll gradually wilt and colour. Season with salt and lots of freshly ground black pepper, and take off the heat.

Slice the salsify at an angle and add to the mushrooms with the radicchio and sorrel, and half the horseradish. Mix the remaining horseradish with the juice of the remaining lemon and the remaining oil to make the dressing.

To serve, divide the salad between 4 plates and lay slices of the beef on top. Mix the dressing together and spoon over the beef.

WARM PORK CHOP, PUMPKIN, TAMARILLO, WATERCRESS, SUNFLOWER AND PUMPKIN SEED SALAD WITH APPLE AND CIDER RELISH

Pork chops are a really succulent cut of meat. While they may have some of that unwanted fat that dieters like to avoid, in this salad they add a juiciness that is very welcome.

I have also used tamarillos in the salad. These were called 'tree tomatoes' when I was a youngster growing up in New Zealand, as they really look like plum tomatoes, hanging down off their tree branches. A native of the Peruvian Andes, they have been grown commercially in New Zealand for as long as I can remember and have become more readily available here in recent years. If you can't locate them then don't panic – replace them with plums or tart nectarines, as what you're after here is a fleshy sour taste.

This way of cooking the seeds is a technique my partner, Michael, has always used when making snacks – they are from his past life as a macrobiotic. Traditionally you cook them without oil, but in this recipe it adds a little moisture to the salad. They are tasty and very addictive.

600g pumpkin, peeled and deseeded

3 tablespoons olive oil, plus more for rubbing the chops

small handful of pumpkin seeds

small handful of sunflower seeds

2 tablespoons soy sauce

salt and freshly ground black pepper

4 large pork chops, each around 200g, on the bone

3 tamarillos (or plums), peeled and each cut into 6

bunch of watercress, thick stalks removed

for the apple cider relish

1 red onion, thinly sliced

1 tablespoon olive oil

2 apples, cored and the flesh cut into 1cm dice

1 tablespoon Demerara sugar

150ml dry cider

100ml cider vinegar

Preheat the oven to 220°C, gas 7. Cut the pumpkin into wedges and place in a roasting tray lined with baking parchment. Season and drizzle with 2 tablespoons of the olive oil, then pour on about ½ cup of hot water and roast until it's cooked through. (You should be able to insert a knife into the thickest part easily when it's cooked.) It will take about 40 minutes, depending on your pumpkin. Thick-fleshed, dense pumpkin will take longer.

Heat a small frying pan and add the remaining oil, then add the seeds and cook over a moderate heat to colour them. Once they're cooked, add the soy sauce. It will steam up, so keep stirring the seeds until it evaporates, then tip on to a tray or plate to cool.

Make the apple and cider relish, sauté the onion in the oil to caramelize it, then add the remaining ingredients. Cook at a rapid simmer until the liquid has almost all evaporated, take off the heat and put to one side.

Season the pork chops and rub with a little extra oil. Heat a heavy pan, skillet, grill or barbecue and cook the chops over a moderate-to-high heat until done. No one I know likes a pork chop cooked anything less than medium well, so keep an eye on it as it cooks. The rule of thumb is to cook it mostly on the first side without turning it over. If the chop is the same as the one I cooked, about 2cm thick, then cook it for 6 minutes on the first side, turn it over and cook for another 3. To see if it's cooked, cut into the thickest part and prise the meat apart: it should be white with a very faint trace of pink. Once rested it will be cooked through. Take off the heat and keep warm.

While the chops are cooking, peel the tamarillo using either a potato peeler or a sharp knife. If using a knife, the best way to peel them is first to remove the stem, then cut them into sixths lengthways and peel the skin away from the flesh slowly and carefully. If using a potato peeler, remove the stem, peel them whole and then cut into 6 lengthways.

To serve, place the still-warm pumpkin on 4 plates. Cut the bone away from the pork and discard (after having a good chew on it), slice the meat reasonably thin and toss with the watercress, the tamarillo wedges and the seeds. Lay this over the pumpkin and spoon on the relish.

Chorizo is one of the great foodstuffs of the world. It is basically minced or chopped pork mixed with pimenton (a smoked paprika) and then cured. It can be fine or coarse, it ranges from lightly spiced to fiery and some doesn't need cooking. However, for this recipe (and the one on page 121) you need to find chorizo perilla – basically 'cooking chorizo'. The onion rings are the sort you'd normally get with steak and chips in an American diner (although these are much tastier) and they add a little bit extra to the salad. If you don't have the time or inclination to make them, then just lay thin slices of raw red onion on the top.

WARM SALAD OF CHORIZO, OLIVE, POTATO, PEAS AND GREEN BEANS WITH ROCKET AND CRISPY ONION RINGS

400g small potatoes

salt and freshly ground black pepper

2 tablespoons white vinegar

600g cooking chorizo (see above)

vegetable oil for deep-frying

1 red onion, sliced into 1cm thick rings

2 tablespoons flour

2 handfuls of beans, blanched and refreshed in iced water

handful of peas, blanched and refreshed in iced water

large handful of olives

2 handfuls of rocket

for the beer batter

175g flour

2 teaspoons sugar

½ teaspoon salt

1 heaped teaspoon baking powder

1 (330ml) bottle of beer

for the dressing

2 tablespoons lemon juice or white wine vinegar

2 tablespoons olive oil

First make the beer batter (as it benefits from at least 20 minutes' resting), sieve the flour, sugar, salt and baking powder together into a bowl, then slowly whisk in the beer. If you add it in a steady stream, you're less likely to get lumps. Leave it to sit for 20 minutes, covered with a cloth or cling film.

Boil the potatoes in plenty of salted water until cooked, then drain. Cut them in half while they are still hot and mix with the vinegar, then leave to cool while you finish the salad.

Peel the skin from the chorizo (it's the casing that holds the meat in place) and slice into rings about 1cm thick. Heat a dry pan and cook the chorizo over a moderate heat to colour the slices on both sides – they sometimes blacken quite quickly, so keep an eye on them. Because the meat is partially 'cured' you can cook it a little rare – you don't need to worry that your guests are going to be fed raw pork so long as you are using a good brand of chorizo.

While the chorizo is cooking, heat a deep-fryer or a pan with 3cm of vegetable oil to 180°C. Separate the onion slices into rings by gently pushing the centres out and toss with the flour, then dip them into the batter, in batches, and gently coat them. Again in batches, cook them in the hot oil until they become golden, being careful not to cook too many at once or they'll stick to each other. Drain on kitchen paper while you cook the rest of them and keep warm.

To make the dressing, mix the lemon juice or vinegar with the olive oil and lightly season.

To serve, toss the potatoes with the beans, peas, olives and rocket, and divide between 4 bowls. Pour over the dressing, then top with the cooked chorizo and the onion rings.

THAI-STYLE BEEF SALAD WITH CORIANDER, MINT, LIME AND PEANUTS

I first ate a salad much like this in Melbourne in 1982, at a Thai restaurant on Brunswick Street, and I was blown away by the freshness of it all. The heat of the chilli was tempered by palm sugar and highlighted by the mint and coriander. It just reeked of 'fresh'... if there's such a thing. Travelling through Thailand 4 years later, I encountered a few different versions, but all with the same basic philosophy of heat, sweet and herbs. I've made this many times over the years and at The Sugar Club restaurant, where I was head chef for many years, I put it on the menu made with kangaroo fillet – it became an instant hit with the customers and remained on even after I left. I've made it using salmon and tuna, and rare-cooked duck as well. It's also excellent as a starter salad (it will serve 6–8 people) or use it as part of an Asian-inspired buffet. You can make it from beef fillet, sirloin or rump steak; it will be as tender as the cut of meat you choose. For this recipe, I have used fillet.

2 teaspoons vegetable oil (groundnut oil works well here)

600g beef fillet (see above), trimmed of all sinew and fat

salt and freshly ground black pepper

3 tablespoons white rice

3 banana shallots, thinly sliced (or use 4–6 regular round shallots)

2 handfuls of roasted, skinless peanuts, roughly chopped (or use the caramelized peanuts on page 10)

handful of mint leaves, stems removed and large leaves torn in half

3 Baby Gem lettuces or 1 large Cos or romaine lettuce

for the coriander and lime dressing

bunch of coriander, ideally with the roots on

1–2 hot red chillies, roughly chopped (more or less to taste, but you do want some fire in this dish)

2 garlic cloves, peeled

1/2 teaspoon salt

finely grated zest of 2 limes and 150ml lime juice (6–8 limes)

2 heaped tablespoons grated palm sugar (or use demerara or brown sugar)

1 teaspoon Thai fish sauce

1 teaspoon soy sauce

Rub the oil all over the beef and lightly season it. Leave to rest for 15 minutes at room temperature on a plate, covered with cling film.

Heat a heavy skillet or grill pan (or even the barbecue). Cook the beef over a quite fierce heat to colour a dark brown on all sides, obviously without burning, then remove from the pan and leave to rest at room temperature for 15 minutes, which will help stop it bleeding when you slice it.

While it's cooking and resting, you can make the dressing with a pestle and mortar or in a small food processor (although the former works better with smaller quantities). If you have the roots of the coriander, then cut them off, discard half and wash the remainder thoroughly (dirt has a way of sticking to them). Roughly chop enough of them to give you a teaspoonful and place in the mortar with the chillies, garlic and salt, and pound to a paste. Finely grate the zest off 2 of the limes, and juice them all, then add the zest to the mortar with the palm sugar and pound again. Add the lime juice, fish sauce and soy sauce, and mix thoroughly to dissolve the sugar. Taste and see if it needs any further sweetness or saltiness, then adjust if necessary by adding either extra palm sugar or fish sauce. Remove the leaves from the coriander stems and cut the stems into 1cm long pieces, then put the leaves and stems in a bowl.

Place the rice in a small pan and cook over moderate heat to colour it pale gold, shaking it often. Once cooked, take it off the heat and allow it to cool, then grind it fairly fine (but not to a powder) in a spice grinder or the mortar.

Once the beef has rested, slice it thinly against the grain and place the slices in a bowl with the shallots, half the peanuts and most of the mint and coriander leaves. Pour on all of the dressing and gently toss together.

To serve, divide the salad leaves among 4 plates and then place the beef salad on top of that. Scatter the remaining peanuts, rice and herbs over as you serve it.

This is a really good winter salad. Beetroot is a much underrated vegetable – I remember when, in 1992, an Australian-chef-led restaurant opened in London's Chelsea and several top reviewers commented on the chef's overuse of beetroot – I think it appeared in two or three dishes. How times change, though. In recent years, restaurants all over the UK have begun to embrace this vegetable anew.

If you buy raw beets, you can cook them in several ways. I prefer to wrap the washed beets tightly in foil and bake at 180°C, gas 4, until you can insert a thin sharp knife into the centre – about 1 hour for a small tennis-ball-sized beetroot. When washing beets, avoid scratching the skin, as they will then bleed their colour. Alternatively, place the beets in a pot, cover with cold water and add 120ml vinegar and 1 teaspoon of salt for every litre of water, then boil until you can almost poke a skewer through them. Either way, peel once cool enough to handle (using gloves, see page 42).

Lightly season the steaks and leave at room temperature, tightly covered with cling film, while you prepare the rest of the ingredients.

Place the parsnips, swede and rosemary in a pot and cover with cold water. Add 1 teaspoon of salt, bring to the boil and cook until the vegetables are tender. Drain in a colander.

Put the pot back on the heat, add the butter and cook it to a 'beurre noisette' stage (i.e. until it is a light nut-brown in colour). Add the thyme, return the vegetables to the pot and coarsely mash them. Season and keep warm.

Finely dice or grate half the beetroot and put in a bowl, then coarsely chop the rest and put in a blender with the garlic, horseradish, vinegar and olive oil. Blitz until smooth. Add this purée to the diced beets and parsley, and mix in. Season well.

Bring a pot of water to the boil, or use a steamer, and briefly cook the spinach, then drain through a colander and gently squeeze out as much excess water as possible. Roughly chop the leaves.

Preheat a grill (or use a heavy pan) and brush the steaks with a little oil on both sides. Assuming your steaks are 1.5cm thick, cook them on a high heat for 3 minutes, then turn over and cook for another 2. This will give you medium-rare steaks; if you want them cooked more or less, then do so. To test how cooked they are, slice into the thickest part of a steak with a sharp knife and look inside. Leave the cooked steaks to rest for 10 minutes in a warm place, such as an oven preheated to 100°C, gas ½, while assembling the dish.

To serve, divide the mashed root veg between 4 plates. Slice the steaks into 1cm thick slices and mix with the spinach, then sit this mix on top. Dollop the beetroot salad over, then drain the onion rings and add them last of all.

SALAD OF GRILLED RUMP STEAK, SPINACH, SMASHED PARSNIPS AND SWEDE WITH BEETROOT, HORSERADISH AND PARSLEY DRESSING

4 rump steaks, each about 200g

salt and freshly ground black pepper

400g parsnips, cut into medium-sized chunks

400g swede, cut into medium-sized chunks

2 tablespoons fresh rosemary leaves

100g butter

1 tablespoon fresh thyme leaves

200g cooked beetroot

1 garlic clove, peeled

2 tablespoons finely grated horseradish (or use horseradish paste)

3 tablespoons red wine vinegar

3 tablespoons extra-virgin olive oil, plus more for brushing

2 large handfuls of flat-leaf parsley

400g spinach

1 red onion, thinly sliced into rings, rinsed in cold water and put in the fridge covered with iced water

This salad is a good hearty meal full of protein. Black pudding may not be to everyone's taste but, if you like it, you'll love this way of serving it. The black pudding we use at The Providores restaurant comes from Stornaway on the Isle of Lewis in Scotland. It's very large – about 7cm in diameter – dry-textured and quite delicious. There are many other black puddings in the UK – Lancashire and Yorkshire are both well known for them – and they are a wonderfully tasty addition to you diet! Mind you, I'm also a fan of haggis, so if that doesn't appeal, then maybe this isn't the recipe for you. However, you can make this salad without one or other of the meats – you could use the vegetable base to go with grilled fish (it would work well with both mackerel and swordfish) or poached chicken, or even serve it as it is, as a vegetable salad.

To make the sage dressing, heat a small pan and add 2 tablespoons of the olive oil. Fry the sage in it until it begins to sizzle, then add the red wine vinegar and the soy sauce and take off the heat. Mix in the remaining oil.

Soft-boil the eggs by bringing a pot of water to the boil and immersing the eggs (best to let them carefully roll off a slotted spoon into the pot). To soft-boil a medium-sized egg, cook it for 4 minutes, then drain and run cold water into the pot for 3 minutes. Shell the eggs.

At the same time as the eggs are cooking, heat a dry pan and cook the black pudding and chorizo until they're done – as they're both fatty they won't need any oil. It may be easier to cook them in batches and keep them warm in an oven preheated to 150°C, gas 2.

While they're cooking, dice the pears and mix with the radishes, broad beans and lemon juice. Season lightly.

To serve, toss the crunchy leaves with the pear salad and divide between 4 plates. Place the cooked meats on top, then rest an egg on top of that – either serve it whole or cut it in half. Spoon the warm dressing over as you serve it.

SALAD OF GRILLED CHORIZO AND BLACK PUDDING WITH SOFT-BOILED EGG, BROAD BEANS, RADISH AND PEAR WITH SAGE DRESSING

4 eggs

250g black pudding, sliced (peeled of any skin or casing)

600g cooking chorizo (see page 115), sliced at an angle

3 pears, cored

12 radishes, thinly sliced

300g broad beans, podded (800g whole bean weight)

2 tablespoons lemon juice

salt and freshly ground black pepper

2 handfuls of crunchy leaves (little Baby Gem or Cos)

for the sage dressing

4 tablespoons extra-virgin olive oil

10 sage leaves, coarsely shredded

2 tablespoons red wine vinegar

2 tablespoons soy sauce

LAMB, MEDJOOL DATE, OLIVE, TOMATO AND FETA SALAD
WITH HONEY DRESSING

This salad reminds me of the salads of Greece and Turkey. It is basically a tomato and feta salad tossed with a few extra bits and pieces, then topped with lamb, and is very quick to knock up and easy to assemble. The honey dressing is a little twist that works well with the acidity of the tomatoes and saltiness of the feta. Try to buy feta made the traditional way, from 100 per cent ewes' milk. You'll find it much tastier than cows'-milk feta.

You can cook the lamb in the oven, as described below, or on a barbecue. At home, I often cook it in a pan. Simply choose a heavy-bottomed pan with a tight-fitting lid and add the lamb when it gets hot. Cook it on a reasonably high heat with the lid on, turning it every minute to cook it evenly. The lid traps in the heat, allows the meat to cook on the top as well as on the bottom, and it keeps the moisture in.

800g lamb loin, trimmed of all fat and sinew

salt and freshly ground black pepper

4 tablespoons extra-virgin olive oil

3 tablespoons runny honey

2 tablespoons cider vinegar

6 plum tomatoes, each cut into 8 wedges

200g feta, cut into large chunks

12 medjool dates, halved and stones removed

4 spring onions, sliced

large handful of olives

large handful of sprouts (see page 16)

juice of 1 lemon

Preheat the oven to 180°C, gas 4. Season the lamb and rub it with a tablespoon of the oil. Heat an ovenproof pan and, when ready, sear the lamb all over, then transfer to the oven and roast for 4–10 minutes. Four minutes will give you medium-rare meat and 10 will give you well done. Keep it warm on a plate in the oven, with the door ajar, while it rests for 10 minutes.

Add the honey and cider vinegar to the still-warm pan and leave it to bubble away, then pour it into a cup with 2 tablespoons of the olive oil and some seasoning – this is your dressing.

Mix the tomatoes, feta, dates, spring onions, olives and the remaining oil together and leave for a minute.

Once the lamb has rested, add the sprouts and lemon juice to the salad and divide among 4 plates.

To serve: slice the lamb into thin pieces and lay this on top of the salad, then spoon on the dressing.

CARPACCIO OF VENISON
WITH SPICED AUBERGINE, LIME AND CUMIN SALAD

While classic Italian carpaccio of beef – thinly shaved raw fillet – is now a familiar dish on modern menus (I have even seen pineapple carpaccio on menus, which I do find a little odd), I also like it when it's made with venison – especially farmed venison, which has a less gamy flavour than its wild forebears. This aubergine salad also teams well with slices of raw fish, and makes a great component of a meal when served tapas- or mezze-style. Restaurants have an advantage over the home cook when slicing meat for carpaccio, as they usually chill the meat until it is almost frozen before slicing it on a commercial meat slicer, but read on and you'll find a more user-friendly approach.

2 red onions, very thinly sliced

finely grated zest of 4 juicy limes and the juice of 2 of them

2 aubergines, stem removed, cut into 2cm dice

vegetable oil, for deep-frying

4 tablespoons extra-virgin olive oil, plus more for drizzling

1 teaspoon cumin seeds

generous pinch of chilli flakes

1 garlic clove, thinly sliced

600g venison fillet, trimmed of all sinew and fat, chilled

small handful of flat parsley leaves

2 spring onions, thinly sliced

1 bunch of coriander, pick off the leaves and finely chop half the stalks as you would chives

Place the sliced onions in a non-reactive bowl with the lime zest and juice and mix well. Cover and chill in the fridge for an hour.

You need to deep-fry the aubergines, so either fill a pan or wok with oil or use a deep-fryer. Heat the oil to 180°C and cook in two batches. Once they turn golden, remove them from the oil and drain well on kitchen paper, then tip into a bowl.

Put the 4 tablespoons of extra-virgin olive oil in a small pan with the cumin seeds, chilli and garlic. Cook until the garlic turns golden, shaking the pan a little as it heats up, then tip out on top of the aubergines. Add the onions with their liquid, together with the parsley and spring onions. Mix lightly.

Place 4 flat plates in the fridge and bring the fillet out. Cut slices from the fillet that are about 1cm thick, put them on another plate and keep in the fridge. Take a length of cling film about 1m long and fold it back on itself to give you a double thickness of 50cm (this makes it somewhat tougher). Alternatively, use a plastic bag or some non-stick parchment. Taking a slice at a time, place the venison in the centre of the plastic, about one-third of the way from the left-hand side, fold the other half over it and begin to gently smash the meat out, working from the centre of the fillet outwards, until uniformly thin.

To serve, cover the base of each of the 4 plates with venison slices, put a mound of the aubergine salad in the centre, scatter with the coriander and finish by drizzling over some more extra-virgin olive oil and sprinkling with salt.

ROSEMARY-CRUSTED LAMB LOIN, CONFIT GARLIC, ROAST TOMATO, SUGAR SNAP AND WATERCRESS SALAD WITH OLIVE AND MINT DRESSING

3 tablespoons fresh rosemary leaves

1 teaspoon coarse salt

10 black peppercorns

3 tablespoons extra-virgin olive oil

800g lamb loin fillet, trimmed of sinew and fat

2 large handfuls of watercress, leaves and only a little of the stem

2 large handfuls of sugar snap peas, blanched and refreshed in iced water

1 lemon, cut into 4 wedges

for the confit garlic

16 garlic cloves, separated but still in the skin

250ml extra-virgin olive oil

for the roast tomatoes

8 medium tomatoes

2 teaspoons extra-virgin olive oil

salt and freshly ground black pepper

for the olive and mint dressing

handful of stoned olives

handful of mint leaves

4 tablespoons lemon juice

This salad can be served warm or cold – you can either cook the lamb at the last minute or cook it a few hours before and then slice it at your leisure. You can also cook the tomatoes and garlic a few days in advance if you want to save time on the day, and then just cook the lamb an hour or two before you need it.

The amount of olive oil used to cook the garlic may seem excessive, but you need to cover all the cloves to cook them properly. Look at it as a way to produce something delicious for other meals, as any leftover oil can be used in a salad dressing or marinade, mixed into mashed potatoes or drizzled over grilled or poached meats.

You can cook the confit garlic in two ways: on the stove or in the oven (the latter is better for larger amounts). To cook it in the oven, preheat it to 170°C, gas 3½. Place the garlic in a small pan and pour on the oil and 100ml water. Bring to the boil, then tip it into a small non-reactive roasting dish just large enough to hold it all comfortably, cover tightly and bake for 90 minutes. It's ready when the garlic cloves can easily be squeezed between your fingers; if they seem a little firm, cook them a bit longer. To cook the garlic on the stove, put the same amount of oil and garlic into a small pot, then add ½ cup of hot water and bring to the boil. Turn down to a very gentle simmer and cook for 45–60 minutes – you need it to bubble away and ultimately for the garlic to gently 'fry' in the oil. It'll be ready when all the water has evaporated.

To make the roast tomatoes, slice the tomatoes across in half and lay on a baking sheet lined with baking parchment. Drizzle the oil over the cut sides, sprinkle with a little salt and pepper, and bake for 1½-2 hours, until the tomato halves have shrivelled a little and are lightly coloured. These can be baked in the oven with the garlic if you're doing it that way. If you're doing them in advance, leave them to cool before storing them in a single layer on a tray in the fridge, tightly sealed with cling film.

Pound the rosemary, coarse salt, peppercorns and oil to a paste using a pestle and mortar, or use a small food processor. Rub this into the lamb and wrap tightly in cling film, then leave to marinate for 1–2 hours.

To prepare the olive and mint dressing, roughly chop the olives and shred the mint. Mix with 3 tablespoons of the garlic cooking oil and leave to one side.

An hour before you plan to eat, turn the oven up to 180°C, gas 4. Heat a heavy ovenproof pan to smoking point, then unwrap the lamb and add it to the pan. Cook for 1 minute each side, then place the pan in the oven and roast for 7 minutes for medium and 10 for medium to well-done. Take from the oven and let rest in a warm (not hot) place for at least 10 minutes before slicing.

To serve, finish the dressing by adding the lemon juice and adjust the seasoning. Mix the confit garlic, watercress, sugar snaps, tomatoes and lamb in a large bowl and divide it between 4 plates, then place the tomato halves on top. Serve the dressing in a bowl and the lemon wedges on the side.

GRILLED FIG, BACON, BORLOTTI BEAN, TOMATO AND MESCLUN SALAD

In August 2004 I was in the Ligurian seaside town of Lerice with my partner, Michael, and our very good friends Stephen and Marina, to celebrate their son Raphael's arrival six months earlier. The beautiful sixties hillside apartment we were staying belonged to Marina's sister and shared a private beach with four others. One morning the gardener arrived with the first figs of the season and a few wild strawberries from the bosco *(the woods from the bushy hill). We served the green figs with slices of lardo (salted and pressed pig's back-fat from Colonnata), some local bitter greens, tomatoes and borlotti beans from the Saturday market on the harbour. Here's a version of that salad.*

Pod the beans and put them in a deep pot, then pour in enough cold water to cover them by 6cm. Bring to the boil and skim off any scum that rises, then add the herbs, onion halves, chilli and garlic, and turn down to a simmer, skimming as necessary. Cook at a rapid simmer for 30–45 minutes until the beans are barely cooked, with a wee bit of bite but not too much. If the cooking liquid falls below the level of the beans, just top up with boiling water from the kettle. Turn the heat off and stir in 1½ scant teaspoons of salt, then leave to cool completely. The beans can be kept in the fridge like this for up to 4 days, so long as they're covered with the cooking liquor.

Drain the beans from the broth and discard all but 2 tablespoons of it, which you can pour back on to the beans. Remove the herbs, scraping the thyme leaves off the stem back into the beans, and squeeze the pulp from the garlic back on to the beans. Cut the tomatoes into a smallish dice and add half to the beans along with 2 tablespoons of the olive oil and some freshly ground black pepper. Mix and put to one side.

Brush a tablespoon of the remaining oil over the cut side of the figs, season with a little salt and pepper, and cook on either a barbecue or a griddle pan, or place under a hot grill, until they caramelize (it is the fructose sugar in them that caramelizes). Take from the heat and put on a warm plate. Grill the bacon until crisp and sit it with the figs.

To serve, squeeze the juice from one of the lemons over the cooked beans and mix well, taste and adjust the seasoning if necessary, then divide the mixture between 4 plates. Cut the other lemon into 4 wedges. Pile the mesclun over the beans and then tuck 3 fig halves into that. Place 2 rashers of bacon on top, then scatter with the remaining tomato dice, drizzle with the remaining oil and serve with a lemon wedge.

700g borlotti beans in the shell
(or any other fresh bean)

10cm sprig of rosemary

1 bay leaf

8 fresh thyme stems

1 small onion, peeled and halved

¼ red chilli, finely chopped

1 garlic clove, unpeeled

salt and freshly ground black pepper

6–8 tomatoes

5 tablespoons extra-virgin olive oil

6 ripe figs, halved lengthways

8 slices of smoked streaky bacon

2 large juicy lemons

2 handfuls of mesclun (mixed salad leaves)

Dessert Salads that provide the perfect finale to any meal

WARM SALAD OF BRIOCHE-HONEY CROUTONS, SAFFRON-POACHED PEAR AND RUM SULTANAS WITH VANILLA MASCARPONE

This warm salad makes a lovely autumn desert and, while the components will take a bit of time to get ready, when the time comes to serve it, it's fairly quick. All the components can be made up to 5 days ahead. If you can't find any brioche, and you don't want to make it yourself, then try something like Madeira cake or panettone treated the same way. For a rich taste, use a honey like a New Zealand Manuka, Tasmanian Leatherwood or a European lavender. This dish is also great when made with quince instead of pear – although these would need cooking almost twice as long as pears.

150g brioche, in any shape or form

4 tablespoons aromatic honey

15g unsalted butter

80g sultanas

3 tablespoons dark rum

6 small or 4 large pears

600ml pear or apple juice

generous pinch of saffron

4 star anise or 4 cloves, or a mixture of the two

¼ vanilla pod

1 tablespoon unrefined caster sugar

100g mascarpone

125ml double cream

You need to prepare the croutons and raisins at least 6 hours ahead. Preheat the oven to 160°C, gas 3, and line a baking tray with non-stick baking parchment. Slice the brioche into pieces about 1cm thick and arrange side by side on the tray. Heat half the honey with the butter and, when it begins to bubble, drizzle it over the brioche. Bake in the middle of the oven until the brioche crisps up and becomes golden, around 20–25 minutes, turning over halfway. If some pieces colour quicker than others, remove and place on a cake rack to cool. Once cool, break into chunks and store in an airtight container.

While the brioche is in the oven, pour a cup of boiling water over the sultanas and leave them to plump up for 20 minutes. Then drain off the water, put the sultanas in a small bowl, pour the rum over them and cover. Ideally, leave them for at least 6 hours to absorb the rum, stirring twice.

Peel the pears, halve or quarter and remove the cores. Place the pieces in a pot just large enough to hold them, pour over the pear or apple juice and the remaining honey, add the saffron and star anise and/or cloves, and bring to the boil. You want the liquid to cover the pears; if there isn't enough, add some boiling water. Place a cartouche (see page 153) or appropriate plate or saucer on top to hold them under the surface and cook at a rapid simmer until you can easily insert a knife through the pears, 20–30 minutes.

Take the cartouche, plate or saucer off the pears, turn the heat up to moderate and cook to reduce the liquid by half, taking care that the pears don't stick to the pan. (If you aren't using them immediately, leave them to cool before storing in the fridge.)

Split the vanilla pod in half lengthways and scrape the seeds into a bowl. Add the sugar and grind together briefly with the back of a spoon (don't discard the pod – it can be used for other recipes). Mix in the mascarpone, then add the cream and whisk until forming medium-firm peaks. Store in the fridge.

To serve, place the pears and syrup in a pan, gently bring to a simmer and cook for 2 minutes. Take off the heat and mix in the sultanas and their juices. Divide the pears and half the sultanas between 4 bowls and scatter the brioche over the top. Dollop on the mascarpone and the remaining sultanas, and pour on all the juice from the pan.

STRAWBERRY, RHUBARB, BLUEBERRY AND MAPLE PECAN SALAD WITH PASSION FRUIT YOGHURT

The range of fruity flavours in this dessert provides a powerful contrast. Rhubarb has a really astringent and strong flavour, blueberries have a sense of denseness in them, and strawberries provide an intense yet light, aromatic flavour. Combined with the vanilla-scented verjuice (the unfermented juice from unripe green grapes, also known by its French name verjus), the whole thing works a treat. The pecans are also good used in savoury salads, so make a big batch and keep in an airtight jar for later use. This fruit salad can be eaten warm or cold and you can use the leftover cooking juices as a cordial – just add sparkling water or tonic.

Preheat the oven to 160°C, gas 3. Toss the pecans with the maple syrup and lay on a tray lined with non-stick baking parchment, then bake for 12–20 minutes, tossing twice to make sure they cook evenly. (They're done when they are golden on the inside – just cut one open after 10 minutes with a knife.) As they cook, the maple syrup evaporates and forms a sweet crust on the outside.

While the pecans are cooking, place the verjuice, sugar and vanilla pod in a medium-to-wide pan. Bring to the boil and then simmer for 5 minutes. Add the rhubarb, ideally in one layer, and bring back to a simmer, then cook it for 4–6 minutes, depending on the thickness. Turn the rhubarb over halfway through, using a fork to flip it. If you overcook the rhubarb, it will begin to break up; if it's a little underdone, it'll just be a bit firmer. Take off the heat.

After 5 minutes, add the blueberries and strawberries, and mix the passion fruit pulp into the yoghurt.

To serve, divide the rhubarb between 4 plates, then spoon over the berries and some of the cooking juices. Dollop on the yoghurt and place a few pecans on top.

large handful of pecan nuts

2 tablespoons maple syrup

350ml verjuice

225g caster sugar

1 vanilla bean, halved lengthways and then halved again

500g rhubarb, cut into 6cm lengths

large handful of blueberries

large handful of strawberries

2 passion fruit, cut in half and pulp removed

200g plain thick yoghurt

This salad can be made from any ripe fruit; it's the addition of the chilli, basil, chocolate sauce and coconut that gives it a surprise lift and makes it a salad for dessert rather than breakfast. Chose 3–5 fruits that are ripe and in season – mango, papaya, mixed berries and banana also work well. I like to crack open a fresh coconut, peel it into thin strips with a potato peeler and toast them (see below), but you can use desiccated coconut instead. Using the fresh coconut may seem like a lot of effort, but you'll be rewarded with delicious, freshly cooked coconut, which really is much better than bought desiccated coconut! Use as much chilli as you can handle – when chilli and sugar are combined, the heat of the chilli feels somewhat lessened, and your tongue senses the flavour of the chilli rather more than the heat.

CHILLIED NECTARINE, PLUM, LYCHEE, PINEAPPLE AND BASIL SALAD WITH CHOCOLATE DRESSING, TOASTED COCONUT

½ medium-hot red chilli, chopped

8 tablespoons caster sugar

2 tablespoons juice and ½ teaspoon finely grated zest from 1 or 2 limes

100g finely grated dark chocolate

3 nectarines, halved, stoned and cut into segments

6 plums, halved, stoned and cut into chunks (I used greengages and red plums)

12 lychees, peeled and stoned

½ sweet baby pineapple, peeled, cored and cut into chunks

8 large basil leaves, torn into small pieces

handful of toasted coconut (see below)

Place the chilli and sugar in a small pan with a cup of water, bring to the boil and simmer for 5 minutes. Take off the heat and divide between 2 bowls. To one bowl, add the lime juice and zest; to the other, add the chocolate. Stir the chocolate into the syrup to blend well and put to one side in a warmish place.

Place all the fruit in a large bowl and pour on the lime syrup, mix well and leave to macerate for 1–2 hours in the fridge, mixing twice.

To serve, take the fruit from the fridge, mix in the basil and divide between 4 bowls. Stir the chocolate dressing and pour it over the fruit, then sprinkle with the coconut.

TO TOAST FRESH COCONUT

Firstly you need to crack open a fresh coconut. Hold it firmly in one hand over a bowl and use either a hammer or the back of a heavy knife. Apply firm blows to crack it open, giving it a quarter turn between hits, bashing it hard in the centre. You will need to turn it a full circle or more to crack it open. At some point you'll hear a hollow thud: this is the shell finally opening up. Prise the two pieces apart using your hands and/or a blunt knife.

Now comes the hard part (and you thought what we've already done was tricky!). I find an oyster knife or large flat screwdriver is best for this. You want to prise the white flesh from the shell, so poke the oyster knife or whatever between both and wiggle it to loosen. Eventually you'll get it all out, but it can

take some time. Alternatively, place the two pieces of coconut in the shell into an oven preheated to 180°C, gas 4, and bake for 30–40 minutes – this will help a little, as the flesh shrinks away from the shell. On no account put an unopened coconut in the oven as they can explode – I have seen this happen at Malaysia's Taipusan festival!

Once you have removed the flesh, shave it thinly using a mandolin grater or potato peeler and arrange in single layers on a few oven trays lined with baking parchment (if it's dumped on in a thick pile, the outer coconut will cook while the inner pieces steam). You can either dust the coconut shreds lightly with icing sugar or cook them as they are, but either way bake at 160°C, gas 3, until golden, keeping

an eye on them as they can go from white and flexible to dark brown and bitter quite quickly. They should be ready within 20–40 minutes. As they become ready (they won't all be ready at the same time) remove them from the tray. Leave to cool and store in airtight containers.

One other piece of advice: occasionally you'll come across a coconut that has gone rotten – not a pleasant sight or smell. It's not always easy to know in advance that this is the case, but when choosing a coconut, make sure it feels dense and you can hear or sense that there is some liquid inside when you shake it. If, on opening it, you are not sure if it's OK (the flesh is grey or rotting, and the smell usually unpleasant), then please just discard it and use desiccated coconut.

PINK GRAPEFRUIT, GRAPE, RASPBERRY AND OLIVE OIL SALAD WITH MINTED YOGHURT

Olive oil in a dessert may seem a little odd, but try to think of it as a flavourful ingredient rather than a fat... as long as you choose a delicious extra-virgin oil. I first had something like this in Jabugo, Spain, when I ate slices of orange simply drizzled with a grassy local oil as a dessert. It was a revelation. If you want to go dairy-free in this dessert, then skip the yoghurt and mix the mint in with the grapes.

2 pink grapefruit

1½ tablespoons extra-virgin olive oil

300g seedless grapes, stems removed

1 teaspoon runny honey

2 handfuls of raspberries

12 mint leaves, finely shredded

240ml thick yoghurt (try a sheep's- or goats'-milk yoghurt for extra flavour)

Peel and segment the grapefruit (see below) over a bowl and reserve any juices that drip from them.

Heat a frying pan and add 2 teaspoons of the oil, then add the grapes and cook over a high heat to blister them slightly, shaking the pan often to cook them evenly. Add the grapefruit juice and cook until it's almost evaporated, then add the honey and bring to the boil. Tip into a bowl and leave to cool.

When the grapes are cool, add the grapefruit segments, raspberries and remaining oil, and gently toss.

Mix the mint into the yoghurt.

To serve, spoon the fruit salad into 4 small bowls and dollop the minted yoghurt on top.

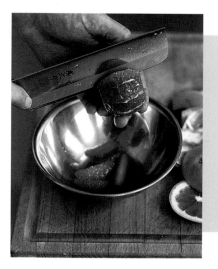

To segment grapefruit (and other citrus fruit): first cut off the top and bottom. Stand it on a cut side and, using a small sharp knife, cut the rind off in downward slices. What you want to end up with looks like a peeled grapefruit with no pith attached, but try not to remove too much flesh. Now hold the fruit in your hand (over a bowl to collect the juices) and carefully remove the segments by slicing into the centre of the fruit, cutting close to the membrane that separates the segments.

GRILLED BANANA AND MANGO SALAD WITH VANILLA-POACHED PEACH

A handy tool to have for this dessert is a small gas burner like the ones they use in restaurants to caramelize crème brûlée – but I won't assume you have one, in which case you'll have to use the grill on your oven, as I did.

When poaching soft fruit like peaches it's important to have enough liquid to keep them suspended above the bottom of the pot, as they can squash a bit once they soften up from cooking. So find a suitable pot – you need them to be able to just fit in it in one layer. If it's too small they'll end up sitting on top of each other; too large and you'll need litres of poaching liquid. Either way, if you find them not floating (you may have jumbo peaches), then just add more liquid. You can poach your peaches up to 4 days ahead, as long as you keep them in their poaching liquor, covered in the fridge.

To make a cartouche, get a square of non-stick baking parchment and sit the lid of the pot on top. Mark with a pen slightly larger than the lid and then cut out a circle. Fold into quarters and snip a 5mm hole from the centre.

Gently wipe the peaches with a damp cloth and, using a very sharp knife, cut a 4cm cross barely through the skin at the pointed end to help the skin come off later (as you would with a tomato for skinning).

Bring the wine, vanilla, sugar, lemon rind and juice to the boil and simmer for 2 minutes. Add the peaches to the pot and bring to the boil, then turn down to a simmer. Place the cartouche (see above, or a suitably sized plate or saucer) on top, press on to the liquid and cook until you can insert a skewer or thin sharp knife into the peaches, about 20 minutes for a ripe medium peach. Leave to cool completely in the liquid.

Take out the cooled peaches one by one and peel the skin from them (you may need to use a knife). Place back in the liquid to store.

Preheat a hot grill. Lay the sliced banana and mango in a single layer on a metal tray lined with lightly oiled foil. Dust with icing sugar, then grill until lightly caramelized.

To serve, make a ring of the grilled fruits on each of 4 plates, then sit a peach in the middle. Drizzle on a few tablespoons of the poaching liquid, sit a piece of lemon rind on top and serve.

4 peaches

1 bottle of white wine (choose the sort of flavours you like – I'd go for a grassy NZ sauvignon blanc or a fruity sweet muscatel, depending on my mood)

1 vanilla pod, halved lengthways and then halved again

225g caster sugar (I like to use unrefined as you get the hint of caramel present)

juice and peeled rind of 1 lemon (peel rind off with a potato peeler or sharp knife avoiding the pith)

2 bananas, peeled and cut at an angle into slices about 1cm thick

1 large mango, peeled, flesh removed from the stone and sliced into 5mm thick pieces

2 tablespoons icing sugar

FIG, DATE, ALMOND, SESAME AND CHOCOLATE SALAD WITH ORANGE ROSEWATER DRESSING

6 figs

8 medjool dates

1 teaspoon runny honey

3 tablespoons rosewater

100ml fresh orange juice

handful of toasted flaked almonds

100g dark chocolate, chopped

1 teaspoon toasted sesame seeds

1 tablespoon almond or hazelnut oil

Fresh figs when fully ripe are incredibly sweet, so I prefer to chill them before eating. As I pen this introduction I am on a gulet (a traditional wide-bodied wooden Turkish boat) off the Dalaman coast with 12 others, blissfully doing nothing more than swimming and writing some of this book. In fact, I am on the deck, under the shade of the sail, having Turkish coffee. The figs we ate for breakfast this morning were more like a sweet syrup encased in a fruity flesh than actual fruit. Medjool dates have a similar quality – rich, sweet flesh. This salad owes some of its inspiration to this trip – the flavours here reminiscent of the fabulous spice bazaar in Istanbul. It is also delicious served with crème fraîche or vanilla ice cream.

You may prefer to peel the figs, but it's not necessary. Remove the woody tip from the stem and cut each fig into 6 wedges, then place these in a bowl.

Cut the dates in half lengthways and pull apart. Remove the stone and the woody bit at the end, and add to the figs.

Stir the honey into the rosewater and orange juice until it's dissolved and pour it over the fruit. Gently mix it all together and place in the fridge for 1–2 hours, mixing once more.

To serve, divide the mixed fruit and juices between 4 plates, scatter over the almonds, chocolate and sesame seeds, and drizzle with the nut oil.

Guide to good greens

If you are lucky enough to have a decent local greengrocer, then try to foster a good relationship with them so that you are not only more likely to get the best of their produce but you can, if necessary, encourage them to source new and unusual leaves and veg for you.

Some of the supermarket chains have recently put a lot of effort into expanding their salad and vegetable lines. Many are now stocking some wonderful delights – even things like pea shoots (in lovely little 'mini greenhouse' packs) and peanut sprouts.

If you are having problems sourcing good interesting salad stuff, then try some of the suppliers here.

SOUTH EAST

G's Marketing
Barway, Ely,
Cambridgeshire CB7 5TZ
tel 01353 727200
salad veg, beetroot, speciality lettuce

Organic Connections International Ltd
Riverdale, Town St, Upwell, Wisbech
Cambridgeshire PE14 9AF
tel 01945 773374
www.organic-connections. co.uk
organic salad veg MAIL ORDER

R&J Salads
Park Hill,
Appledore, Ashford,
Kent TN26 2BJ
tel 01233 758224
salad veg, herbs, specializing in unusual salad leaves and pea shoots
not organic but use minimum chemicals and no artificial fertilizers

Remfresh
Mansards, Harts Lane, Ardleigh, Colchester,
Essex CO7 7QH
tel 01206 230144
baby veg and speciality lettuces

Secretts
Hurst Farm,
Chapel Lane,
Milford, Godalming,
Surrey GU8 5HU
tel 01483 520500
baby leaves and other salad veg
www.secretts.co.uk MAIL ORDER

MIDLANDS

Aconbury Sprouts
Unit 4, Westwood Industrial Estate,
Pontrilas, Hereford HR2 OEL
tel 01981 241155
salad veg, sprouted seeds specialists

FletcherSalads
Gedney Broadgate,
Spalding, Lincolnshire
PE12 0DG
tel 01406 363206
unusual salad leaf specialists

Jack Buck Growers
Oak House Coldstores,
Holbeach Bank, Spalding,
Licolnshire PE12 8BL
tel 01406 422615
specialty salad veg

Ryton OrganicGardens
Ryton-on-Dunsmore,
Coventry, West Midlands CV8 3LG
tel 024 7630 8201
www.hdra.org.uk
organic salad veg

SOUTH WEST

Jekka's Herb Farm
Rose Cottage,
Shellards Lane,
Alveston, Bristol,
BS35 2SY
tel 01454 418878
salad herbs MAIL ORDER

SOUTH

Sunnyfields Organic Farm
Jacobs Gutter Lane, Totton,
Southampton SO40 9FX
tel 023 8087 1408
www.sunnyfields.co.uk
A wide range of organic salad vegetables, herbs and sprouted seeds

NORTH OF ENGLAND

Howbarrow Organic Farm,
Howbarrow Farm,
Cartmel, Grange-over-Sands
Cumbria LA11 7SS
tel 01539 536330
www.howbarroworganic.demon.co.uk
organic salad veg MAIL ORDER

WALES

Llwynhelyg Farm Shop
Sarnau, Llandysul,
Ceredigion SA44 6QU
tel 01239 811079
Fresh herbs and salad leaves

SCOTLAND

Kingscross Herbs
Grays Cottage,
Kingscross,
Ayrshire KA27 8RG
tel 01770 700 586
Organically grown fresh herbs and salad vegetables
MAIL ORDER

Strathspey Mushrooms Ltd
Unit 12,
Dalfaber Industrial Estate.
Aviemore,
Inverness-shire PH 22 1PY
tel 01479 810583
Mushrooms and truffles

NORTHERN IRELAND

Farm Fresh Fruit & Vegetables
47 Dobbin Rd, Portadown,
Armagh BT62 4EY
tel 028 3833 2918
Fresh herbs and salad vegetables

Index

ACKNOWLEDGEMENTS

A huge thank you to my partner Michael for all his ongoing fantastic support.

Thanks also to the entire team at The Providores for their generous assistance and inspiration.

Finally, I would like to acknowledge the significant contribution made by the entire team who worked on the book: Jane O'Shea for commissioning it, Lewis Esson for editing it so sympathetically, Jean Cazals for his brilliant photographs, Lawrence Morton for his impeccable design, Sue Rowlands for her elegant styling and, last but by no means least, my agent Felicity Rubinstein.

Medley Salads

that make use of an assortment of types of added protein

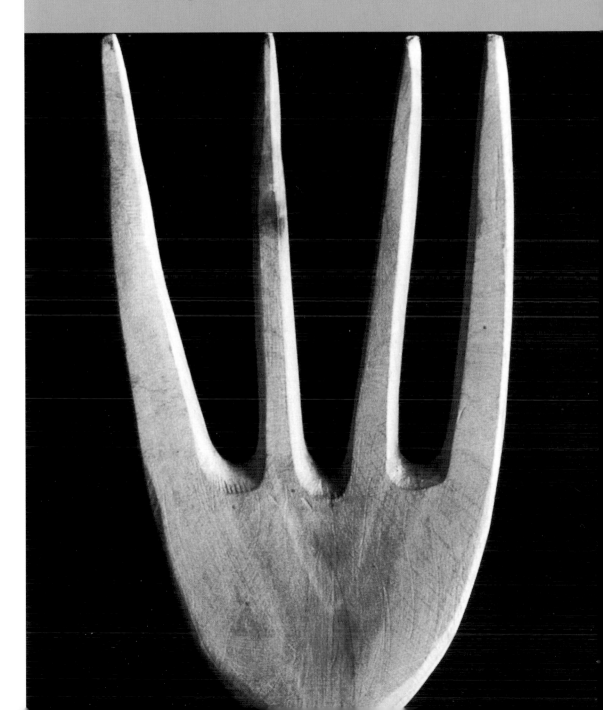

CHICKEN, PRAWN, AVOCADO, PECAN AND MANGO SALAD WITH BABY GEM, WATERCRESS AND SPROUTS

This is another one of those 'what's in the fridge' sorts of salads. It doesn't require lots of measuring, or making sure everything's perfectly weighed out. You could cook a chicken specially or you could just go and buy one ready-cooked. You can use a poached, steamed, roasted or grilled chicken – it won't matter too much. Likewise, you can either cook raw prawns from scratch or simply buy ready-cooked ones.

1 large cooked chicken

2 avocados

1 large mango

12–20 (depending on size and appetite) peeled cooked prawns

large handful of pecan nuts, toasted

3 Baby Gem lettuces, leaves separated

bunch of watercress, thicker stems removed

2 tablespoons lemon juice or cider vinegar

3 tablespoons avocado oil

salt and freshly ground black pepper

handful of sprouts (see page 16)

Remove the flesh from both the breasts and the legs of the chicken, and either break it or cut it into chunks, then put in a large bowl.

Cut the avocados in half and remove the stone, then scoop out the flesh, cut it into chunks and add to the chicken.

Peel the mango and cut both cheeks from the stone, cut these into chunks and add to the chicken with the prawns, pecans, Baby Gem leaves and watercress.

Make the dressing by mixing the lemon juice with the avocado oil and seasoning lightly.

To serve, toss the salad gently with half of the dressing, then divide between 4 plates and scatter with the sprouts. Drizzle on the remaining dressing.

Squid and chorizo is a combination I've written about before in another book and one I just adore. The rich oiliness of the chorizo, highlighted with the spicy notes of pimenton (Spanish smoked paprika), goes so well with the almost blandness of the squid. There are basically two types of chorizo: those intended to be cooked and those to be served thinly sliced as you would a salami. For this recipe, you want the former. From this you'll need to choose from spicy (picante) or less spicy and a little sweet (dulce).

Arame is a type of black seaweed from Japan, usually bought dried, that is easy to use and available from health food shops and Japanese food stores. You can substitute hijiki or other dried or fresh seaweeds.

For this recipe, I've used canned cannellini beans. If you want to cook them from scratch, simply pod them and cook in lots of boiling water, adding salt just before they become al dente. This salad can be served both hot and cold.

HERB AND OLIVE-OIL-POACHED SQUID SALAD
WITH CHORIZO, CANNELLINI BEANS, ARAME, SUGAR SNAPS AND BABY POTATOES

small handful of dried arame (see above)

1 tablespoon soy sauce

600g medium-sized squid (heads 12-15cm long), cleaned (see left)

2 medium red onions, sliced into rings

150ml extra-virgin olive oil

1 red chilli, thinly sliced

2 tablespoons fresh thyme leaves

1 tablespoon oregano

2 bay leaves, halved

10 garlic cloves, sliced

salt and freshly ground black pepper

5 tablespoons lemon juice

400g tin of cannellini beans, drained

300g cooking chorizo sausages (see above), sliced at an angle 5mm thick

large handful of sugar snap peas, blanched and refreshed in iced water

300g baby potatoes or a variety like Anya, Pink Fir or La Ratte, cooked and drained

handful of flat-leaf parsley

Place the arame and soy sauce in a small heatproof bowl, barely cover with boiling water from the kettle and leave to rehydrate, around 30 minutes.

To clean the squid you can do one of two things: the easiest is to get your fishmonger to clean it; otherwise, you'll need to do it yourself – which is actually quite a nice tactile job. Pull the tentacles and guts from the hood-shaped head in one piece. You'll notice the eyes on this – cut the tentacles from just below them. Pull the tentacles apart, removing the beak at the same time. (The beak is located in the centre of the tentacles – just squeeze it out and discard.) Put the tentacles in one bowl. Peel the thin membrane from the outside of the head and pull the fins off, then peel these as well. Insert a sharp knife into the head and slice it open – to give you a large triangular flap. Cut this into thin strips like spaghetti. Slice the fins the same size and put in another bowl.

Sauté half the onion rings in a large pot with all but 2 tablespoons of the oil and, when they wilt, add the chilli, herbs and half the garlic. Continue cooking over a moderate-to-high heat, stirring frequently, until the garlic colours.

At the same time, bring a large pot of lightly salted water to the boil and drop in the squid tentacles. Count to 10, then add the sliced head and fins. Give it a stir, count to 5 and then drain through a colander.

Add the squid to the onions and increase heat to moderate. Cook for a minute, stirring frequently. Season and mix in half the lemon juice. Take off the heat.

Add the remaining 2 tablespoons of oil to a hot pan and caramelize the remaining onion and garlic in it. Add the drained cannellini beans and ½ cup of cold water. Bring to the boil and simmer for 5 minutes. Taste and adjust the seasoning, then put to one side.

Grill or fry the chorizo, without oil, for a minute or so on both sides – it'll char slightly, but this isn't a bad thing. Keep warm while you finish the salad. Slice the sugar snaps at an angle and cut the potatoes in half if large.

To serve, mix the beans with the parsley and potatoes, and divide between 4 plates, then lay the chorizo on top. Toss the squid with the drained arame, sugar snaps and reserved lemon juice, and divide this among the plates.

SALAD OF BACON LARDONS, CHÈVRE, OVEN-DRIED TOMATOES AND GRAPES, WITH AVOCADO, CRÈME FRAÎCHE, TARRAGON DRESSING

Neither too light nor too heavy a meal, this salad makes a great summer brunch, but is also lovely served warm in autumn. If you don't eat bacon, then you could simply not add it to the salad or replace it with cooked prawns, chicken or even sautéed wild mushrooms. If you are able to source unsliced smoked bacon then all the better – take the rind off and cut into 5mm thick slices. Then lay 4 slices on top of each other at a time – and cut these into 5mm thick batons. If you can only find sliced bacon, then no problems, just cut the rind off and cut into 5mm wide pieces.

Chèvre is the French term for goats' cheese that you'll find either as fat round 'buttons' or in log shapes. It usually has a white rind (although there are many varieties, including a popular one that has a black rind from being rolled in ash) and a crumbly white interior. If you're no fan of goats' cheese then shame on you – but being the forgiving chef that I am, you can replace it with almost any crumbly cheese, just don't use something like Cheddar.

8 ripe medium-sized tomatoes, halved

3 garlic cloves, very thinly sliced

6 tablespoons extra-virgin olive oil or avocado oil

salt and freshly ground black pepper

2 large handfuls of grapes, removed from the stem

300g chèvre (see above)

300g smoked bacon batons (see above)

1 large avocado, halved, stone removed and flesh scooped out

2 tablespoons lemon juice

100ml crème fraîche

3 tablespoons fresh tarragon leaves (just pull them off the stem)

2 large handfuls of mixed salad leaves (anything will do here, so take your pick from frisée, oak leaf, rocket, watercress, chicory or dandelion, or use a mixture of many)

Preheat the oven to 170°C, gas 3½, and line a baking dish with baking parchment. Lay the tomato halves on this, cut side up. Divide the garlic slices among the tomatoes, then drizzle them with 1 tablespoon of the oil, season lightly and place in the oven for an hour.

Toss the grapes with another tablespoon of the oil and add to the baking dish then cook both tomatoes and grapes for a further 30 minutes. By now the tomatoes should have shrivelled a little – the grapes likewise. If the tomatoes colour too quickly, take them out, or turn your oven down.

Cut the chèvre into 1cm chunks (it may crumble, so they needn't be perfect cubes) and place a piece on each tomato half. Turn the oven off and keep them warm. Put the remaining chèvre into a bowl.

Heat a frying pan, add another tablespoon of the oil, then add the bacon lardons and cook over a moderate-to-high heat to colour and crisp them, stirring frequently to prevent them catching or burning. Once cooked, drain on kitchen paper and keep warm.

Mash or purée the avocado with the remaining olive oil, lemon juice, crème fraîche and half the tarragon. You can do this in a small food processor or blender, or using a firm whisk. Season and put to one side.

To serve, divide the tomatoes between 4 plates and sit the salad leaves on top. Dollop on the avocado mixture, reserving a little for your guests to top up. Toss the still-warm grapes with the remaining chèvre and bacon lardons, and place this on the salad, then scatter with the remaining tarragon.

WARM SALAD OF DUCK CONFIT, BUTTER BEANS AND GRILLED CHORIZO
ON WILTED SPINACH AND ROAST SWEET POTATO WITH CAPE GOOSEBERRIES

This salad is definitely one for the autumn and winter. The flavours are earthy and the ingredients rich – it's salad as comfort food. Duck confit is best described as duck cooked in its own fat, which may sound a bit much, but it is, in fact, a delicious moist product. The duck is cooked very slowly over several hours, rendering it tender and juicy. Once it's reheated in the oven it becomes 'fall off the bone' delicious, which is handy as you do want to take it off the bone. You should be able to buy duck confit from a French deli or larger supermarkets.

To make this salad even more convenient to knock up, I used a jar of jumbo plump Spanish butter beans, which are also rich and satisfying, and vacuum-packed whole chestnuts. The cape gooseberries add a tart note as you bite into them and the brandy dressing gives an aroma that, combined with the rest of the ingredients, really makes this a meal to enjoy when it's cold outside.

2 medium-to-large sweet potatoes (I used New Zealand kumara, which were fantastic), unpeeled and sliced into 2cm thick rounds

salt

4 duck confit legs

500g spinach

250g chorizo sausages, suitable for cooking, sliced at an angle 1cm thick

150g chestnuts (use vacuum-packed ones)

200g (drained weight) cooked butter beans

3–4 good slugs of brandy (or try a good dark rum or whisky)

large handful of cape gooseberries (physalis fruits)

Preheat the oven to 180°C, gas 4, and line a large roasting dish with baking parchment. Place the sweet potato slices in a large pot of boiling salted water and cook until you can almost poke a wooden skewer through. Carefully lift them out of the water and let rest on a plate.

Place the duck, skin side up, in the lined roasting dish with any of the fat that may be clinging to it and roast for 20 minutes. After 5 minutes, add the sweet potato slices and season them well.

While these are cooking, blanch the spinach and drain – don't refresh.

Heat a wide frying pan and add the chorizo, trying to keep it in one layer so that it cooks evenly. Once the slices have coloured on one side, turn them over and colour on the other side, then move to one side of the pan and add the chestnuts. Sauté these to colour them lightly, then add the butter beans and brandy, and cook until most of the liquid has evaporated. Add the spinach to the pan and toss everything together.

To serve, divide the roasted sweet potato between 4 plates and sit the spinach salad on top. Turn the duck legs over and pull the bones out from the leg – there will be the thigh bone, the leg bone and, occasionally, a smaller bone that doesn't always come out with the other two. If you don't want to eat the skin, then flip the leg back the other way and peel it off – it should come away easily. Otherwise, just pull the leg apart into chunks and lay these on the salad. Tuck the gooseberries into the salad and serve while still warm.

This salad is totally delicious – Lewis, the editor of this book, and I scoffed it down after it was photographed and it makes an elegant meal. If you're no fan of oysters, you could make it from prawns or scallops, and if you're no fan of raw beef then you could make it from roast beef. However, it will not be quite as satisfactory and quite so fantastic. The oysters I used were huge – so three each were just enough. If you're a big fan of them, like my father, Bruce, then you may need to serve more. I used Greek cress in this dish – if you can't find any, replace it with watercress or rocket – something peppery is good. If you are deep-frying the oysters in a pot or pan (rather than a purpose-made deep-fryer), use a deep-sided pot. This will stop it spitting and splattering so much, and I find them a little safer than a shallow pan. However, what I always use at home is a wok – set on a secure wok base.

SALAD OF BEER-BATTERED OYSTERS, GREEK CRESS, SHIITAKE MUSHROOMS AND CRISPY LEEKS ON RAW BEEF WITH GINGER DRESSING

First prepare the ginger dressing, cut the ginger into fine julienne strips and mix with the rice vinegar and a pinch of salt. Cover and leave to marinate for 30 minutes.

Meanwhile, make the beer batter, sieve the flour, salt, sugar and baking powder into a bowl. Using a whisk as you pour, mix in the beer in a steady stream. If you keep mixing, you should get no lumps. Cover and put to one side.

Sauté the mushrooms in 2 tablespoons of the olive oil to wilt them, then mix in the sesame oil and take off the heat.

Slice the beef fillet against the grain into round slices about 2–3mm thick and lay these on 4 plates, spreading them out, then cover each plate with cling film and keep to one side away from any heat.

Cut the leek lengthways in half, then lay each half on a chopping board, cut side down, and cut into long thin strips.

Take the oysters out of their shells, or get them shucked by your fishmonger and lay on kitchen paper to remove excess moisture.

Heat the oil for deep-frying to 160°C. Add half the leek and cook, gently stirring to keep it cooking evenly, until it becomes golden. Should it go as far as dark brown, it will become bitter, while not cooked enough and it will be limp and tasteless. Remove the leek with a slotted spoon and drain on kitchen paper. Cook the remaining leek in the same way.

Increase the temperature of the oil to 180°C. Place 4 of the oysters in the batter and very gently coat them in it, then lower them into the oil. Cook until golden all over (if your oil is shallow, you'll need to turn them over after a minute), then remove with a slotted spoon and drain on kitchen paper while you cook the rest. Keep the cooked ones warm in a low oven with the door ajar. The oysters will spit a little as they cook – they are juicy creatures after all, so please do be careful as you cook them.

To serve, place a mound of Greek cress in the centre of the beef slices and scatter the shiitake and ginger, with the marinating vinegar, around it. Tuck 3 oysters into the cress and then lay the leeks on top. Drizzle with the remaining olive oil and serve.

16 shiitake mushrooms, stems removed and caps sliced

3 tablespoons olive oil

1/2 teaspoon sesame oil

500g beef fillet, trimmed of any sinew and fat

10cm cut from the middle of a fat leek

12 large oysters

vegetable oil for frying at a depth of at least 3cm

handful of Greek cress

for the ginger dressing

1 fat finger of peeled ginger

4 tablespoons rice vinegar, lemon juice or cider vinegar

salt

for the beer batter

120g flour

1/2 teaspoon salt

1 1/2 teaspoons sugar

1/2 teaspoon baking powder

250ml beer

REVOLUTIONARY RUSSIAN SALAD
OF POTATOES, CARROTS, BEANS, PEAS, TONGUE, TRUFFLE AND LOBSTER

While the classic Russian salad – first created by French chefs at the courts of the Tsars – may just seem too odd a combination, it is actually quite a delicious dish. It is an example of a European salad with contrasting textures and a complex array of ingredients – while truffle and lobster may seem happy to sit on the same plate, truffle oil and ox tongue are a revelation.

With the usual mayonnaise binding replaced by a lemon vinaigrette, you will find this much lighter and fresher than the Russian salad of memory. I've assumed that most people will find it hard to get hold of a few slices of fresh white truffle, so truffle oil comes to the rescue. And for those of you still a little squeamish about tongue, substitute some crispy grilled pancetta or even some sliced roast chicken breast.

2 lobsters, each about 500g, cooked and flesh removed (see below)

350g waxy potatoes (Anya, Fingerling and Pink Fir are good choices), boiled and cooled

large handful of green beans

150g fresh peas, blanched

8 thickish slices (about 200g) of cooked and peeled ox tongue, or use lambs' tongues

12–16 baby carrots (or use a large carrot cut into batons)

small bunch of sprouts (page 16) or cress

for the dressing

1½ teaspoons white truffle oil (black truffle oil has an earthier flavour that doesn't work so well here)

2 tablespoons extra-virgin olive oil

2 tablespoons lemon juice

salt and freshly ground black pepper

Slice the lobster tail across into 8 pieces. If the digestive tract is still intact (it runs through the centre of the tail), pick it out of each slice with a toothpick. Cut the potatoes in half lengthways. Blanch the green beans and peas in boiling water for 2 minutes only, and then refresh in cold water until cool.

Make the dressing by mixing the truffle oil, olive oil and lemon juice, and lightly season.

To serve, interweave the lobster tail and tongue slices on the plate, and drizzle with a few teaspoons of the dressing. Mix the potatoes, carrots, beans and half the remaining dressing in a bowl and place on top, scattering the peas over last of all. Place a shelled lobster claw on top, then pour the remaining dressing over and scatter with the sprouts or cress.

Cooking lobster

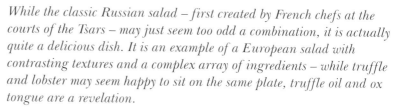

The most humane way to cook a live lobster is first to wrap it tightly in a plastic bag and place it in the freezer for 2 hours, as this puts it into a comatose state. Meanwhile, two-thirds fill a pot large enough to hold your lobster comfortably with cold water. Add a handful of herbs, such as bay, thyme, coriander root, oregano etc., a sliced small onion and carrot and 1½ teaspoons of fine sea salt for every litre of water. Bring to the boil, add your chilled lobster, hold it under the water for 20 seconds, then boil for 5 minutes for the first 500g and 3 minutes for every further 500g. Remove from the pot, put into a bowl of iced water for 1 minute, then leave to cool completely.

Get your hammer and claw crackers out and gently smash the shell as you pull out the flesh from the claws and head. The tail is somewhat easier to attack by wrapping it in a tea towel and firmly twisting it from the head as you would wring out a towel. Gently but firmly pull it away from the head. Take a pair of kitchen scissors and cut along the smooth side (the belly) of the tail on either side. Now prise the shell away from the flesh and you will eventually get a whole tail of meat. You should now have the tail, two claws and a pile of loose meat.

CRISPY PANCETTA, ROAST COD, BROAD BEAN AND ORANGE ROAST FENNEL SALAD

Pancetta and panceta are respectively the Italian and Spanish terms for cured pork belly, much like bacon – and the Spanish version is usually also rubbed with pimenton (smoked paprika) before it is cured. Both styles are much firmer than bacon and will go very crisp when cooked. If you can, buy a slab of it and slice it yourself; however, if you're not too keen on the idea, then get your deli to do it for you.

Always buy cod that has been fished in a sustainable manner – your fishmonger should be able to tell you if it has. If no cod is available, then you can replace it with most other fish; but for this dish you want to use something with flesh that breaks into large flakes – try salmon, sea trout, large snapper, pollock or haddock. This salad can be served warm or cold.

Preheat the oven to 180°C, gas 4. Trim both ends off the fennel and slice the heads across into 3mm rings. Peel the rind off the orange, avoiding the pith underneath (or use a citrus zester, which is made just for this one job), then cut it into fine julienne strips. Juice the orange.

Place the fennel, orange zest and juice in a non-reactive roasting dish (ideally a ceramic one) and drizzle on a third of the oil. Season and bake until the fennel has wilted and begun to colour a little, tossing it once after about 20 minutes. It should take about 35 minutes in all.

You can cook the pancetta in one of two ways. The first is to lay it on a cake rack above a baking tray and bake in the bottom of the oven while the fennel is cooking until it goes very crisp, around 40 minutes; the second is to cook it slowly in a non-stick pan until crisp.

Rub half the remaining oil over the flesh side of the cod and season it. Lay it in a roasting dish lined with baking parchment, skin side down, and roast until just cooked – check it after 8 minutes, as the exact cooking time will depend on the size of the pieces. The cod is cooked when you can separate the flesh using a small sharp knife – it should be a little opalescent.

Mix the broad beans with the dill, the remaining olive oil and the lemon juice.

To serve, place the chicory on 4 plates and scatter the fennel over. Once the cod has cooled sufficiently for you to handle it, flake it apart and divide over the fennel. Add the bean and dill salad with any of their juices, then lastly lay the pancetta on top.

3 medium heads of fennel

1 large orange

6 tablespoons extra-virgin olive oil

200g thinly sliced pancetta, rind removed

800g cod fillets, pin bones removed

2 large handfuls of broad beans, cooked and podded

small handful of dill, cut into 2cm lengths

3 tablespoons lemon juice

2 heads of chicory, leaves separated